# A GUIDE TO FRESH- AND SALT-WATER
# FISHING
a Golden Guide® from St. Martin's Press

by
**GEORGE S. FICHTER**
and
**PHIL FRANCIS**
under the editorship of Herbert S. Zim

Illustrated by
**TOM DOLAN, KEN MARTIN**
and
**HARRY McNAUGHT**

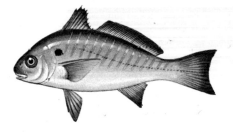

St. Martin's Press    New York

# FOREWORD

This basic guide to sport fishing is designed to give the beginning fisherman a proper start and to be a useful and interesting reference to anglers of long experience. It describes the principal fishes taken on hook and line in fresh and salt waters throughout North America and provides information also about the tackle and techniques for catching fish.

We appreciate greatly the help and advice given by our many fisherman friends and most particularly by Morrie Upperman, of Bill Upperman's Bucktails; James D. Barhydt, of E. I. du Pont de Nemours & Co.; D. C. Corkran, of the Charles F. Orvis Co.; Richard H. Davimos, of Harrison Industries, Inc.; Charles B. Dunn, Jr., of Southern Tackle Distributors, Inc.; Robert G. Martin, of the Sport Fishing Institute; E. B. Maguire, of True Temper Corporation; Ronald J. Holtz, of James Heddon's Sons; G. G. Smith, of the Enterprise Manufacturing Co.; and W. J. Laurent, of Shakespeare Co.

PHOTO CREDITS: Three Lions, p. 4; APA, p.5; Michigan Tourist Council, p. 130; Florida State News Bureau, pp. 134, 135, 139, 149; Ed Gallob, p. 138; Bertram Yacht Div., Nautec Corp., p. 142 (top); Arkansas Publicity and Parks Commission, p. 142 (bottom); Larry Koller, p. 144.

# CONTENTS

## SPORT FISHING

Sport fishing—catching fish for fun—began in ancient times. Man fished first for food, of course, then made a sport of it. Primitive man used a gorge, forerunner of today's fishhook. It consisted of a piece of bone, wood, or shell sharpened at both ends. A line was tied to its center, and the gorge was hidden in a bait. When a fish swallowed the morsel, the line was pulled tight, lodging the gorge crosswise in the fish's gullet.

Barbed hooks are mentioned in the Bible, and the Red Hackle, an artificial fly first described by the Romans, is still used to this day. By 1496, when Dame Juliana Berners, a Benedictine nun, published "The Treatyse of Fysshynge wyth an Angle" in *The Book of St. Albans*, fishing had definitely become a sport.

Then came Izaak Walton, patron saint of modern fishing, whose classic book, *The Compleat Angler*, first appeared in 1653. A truly contemplative angler, Izaak Walton enjoyed a day by the stream as much as the catch. His descriptions of the art of fishing are still inspiring.

Approximately 30 million fishing licenses are sold annually in the United States, and an estimated 30 million additional anglers fish where licenses are not required, as in most salt-water fishing areas. Every year anglers take some 500 million pounds of fish from fresh waters and about 700 million pounds from salt. Roughly 25 billion dollars are spent annually on this popular sport. In the United States, there are some 100,000 lakes and more than a million miles of streams and rivers for the freshwater fisherman and more than 90,000 miles of coastline on which the salt-water fisherman can try his luck. Most important is the immeasurable pleasure enjoyed by each of these millions of fishermen.

# FISHES

Fishes are a varied group of some 40,000 species, most of which have skeletons of bone. The few hundred species of sharks, rays, and lampreys have skeletons of cartilage. Most bony fishes are covered with overlapping scales over which there is a thin skin that secretes a coating of slime. This aids the fish in slipping through the water and protects it from parasites. A fish's age can be determined by counting the rings on its scales. The typical fish has two sets of paired fins (pectoral and pelvic) and three un-paired fins (dorsal, anal, and caudal). It swims mainly by wagging its body from side to side and uses its fins for steering. A fish breathes by alternately opening its mouth to let in water, then shutting its mouth and forcing the water back over its gills and out the gill openings. As the water passes over the gill filaments, dissolved oxygen is exchanged for carbon dioxide.

**PARTS OF A FISH**

Detail of Scale

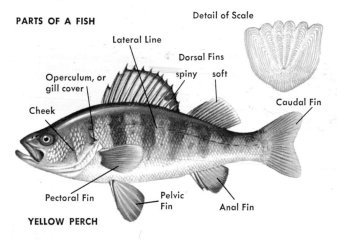

Lateral Line

Dorsal Fins

spiny    soft

Operculum, or
gill cover

Caudal Fin

Cheek

Pectoral Fin

Pelvic
Fin

Anal Fin

**YELLOW PERCH**

6

A fish's shape is a clue to where it lives, how it feeds and the sort of fight it puts up when hooked. Fish of the open sea generally have a spindle-shaped body. They depend on speed to escape enemies and to catch food. They fight hard. Many kinds leap from the water as they try to get rid of the hook. Marlins, tunas and mackerels are among these fast, streamlined fish.

At the opposite extreme are flat or chunky bottom-dwellers. Usually slow swimmers, they do not jump when hooked, but may pull hard as they bore deeper into the water. Some will saw the line in two on pilings or rocks.

Many fish that live in quiet waters between the surface and the bottom have a compressed body—flattened from side to side. Members of the sunfish family in fresh water or pompanos, among others, in salt water are of this type.

Many fishes are protected from enemies by sharp spines or spiny fins, some of which are poisonous. A puffer can inflate its body until it is too large for a predator to swallow. Groupers and flounders are among the fish that can change their color or pattern so that they blend with their surroundings.

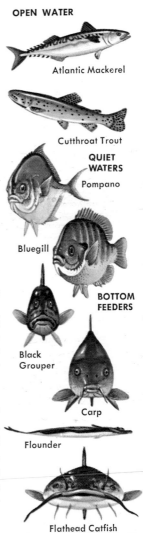

**OPEN WATER**

Atlantic Mackerel

Cutthroat Trout

**QUIET WATERS**

Pompano

Bluegill

**BOTTOM FEEDERS**

Black Grouper

Carp

Flounder

Flathead Catfish

# SENSES

Fish detect danger and find their food by their senses of sight, hearing, smell, and taste. Generally, fish with a well-developed sense of sight are predators; they eat smaller fish or other live, active animals. Their sense of smell is not as well developed as it is in bottom feeders, many of which are scavengers.

## SIGHT

A fish's eyes are at the sides of its head; hence it can see behind as well as in front. Experiments have demonstrated that many fish can detect even slight variations in form and that they can see colors ranging over the spectrum from red to violet. Fresh-water bass, for example, often show strong preference for lures that are red or yellow. A fish can focus on near objects and can detect even slight movements in distant objects. Distance vision is limited by the short range light travels in water. Fish that live at moderate depths or those that feed in dim evening or morning light may have large eyes. Fish that find their food mainly by its odor, as do catfish and eels, have small eyes. Fish that feed mainly by sight readily take artificial lures (p. 66).

Left Eye Only

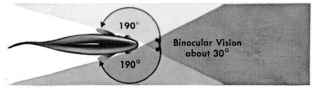

190°

Binocular Vision about 30°

190°

Right Eye Only

Light rays bend in passing from water to air; hence fish's exact location varies with observer's viewing angle.

A fish looks from the water through a circular window, which varies in size with the clarity of the water and the fish's depth.

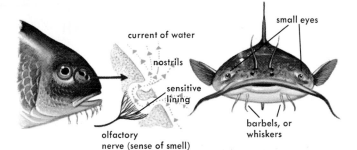

current of water

nostrils

sensitive lining

small eyes

olfactory nerve (sense of smell)

barbels, or whiskers

**HEARING** Vibrations travel more rapidly and also greater distances in water than in air. Lures that gurgle, pop, or rattle attract a fish's attention; they can be "heard" without being seen and are effective at night or in murky water where silent lures pass unnoticed. Fish do not hear fishermen talking because these sound waves are in the air, but banging on a boat sets up vibrations in the water that may frighten fish away. A fish picks up vibrations through the ear bones in its skull; it has no external ear openings. Its lateral line, with pores opening to the outside, detects low-frequency vibrations, such as footsteps on the bank, and changes in pressure or current direction.

**SMELL AND TASTE** are closely related, but smell is effective at a distance, while an object must be contacted to be tasted. A fish's nostrils are blind sacs lined with a tissue that is sensitive to odors. At spawning time, salmon find their way from the sea to their parental stream by the odor of its water. They can be guided to a new spawning area by an odor path of the old stream. Odors given off by alarmed or injured minnows attract predators. Thus, a bass may seek a wounded (hooked) minnow used for bait. Taste organs on the whiskers or barbels help catfish, drums, and others find food. Natural baits, especially those with a strong odor (p. 58), work best for these fish.

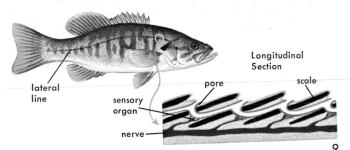

lateral line

sensory organ

nerve

Longitudinal Section

pore

scale

# SPORT FISH

Brown Trout

Largemouth Bass

Bluegill

Any fish that is fun to catch on hook and line qualifies as a sport fish. Opinions vary about which fish are the most game, however. A 14-inch Smallmouth Bass, a prize catch to a Midwest fisherman, might be scorned by a Florida fisherman accustomed to battling Tarpon or a California fisherman who catches Albacore. Most fishermen agree that salt-water fish show more speed, strength, and stamina than do freshwater fish.

Gameness varies, too, with habitat and climate. Largemouth Bass caught in cool northern lakes often fight harder than Largemouths of the same size from warm southern lakes. Walleyes taken from rivers battle much harder than do Walleyes from lakes. But extra size may make up for the difference, as Largemouth Bass grow larger in the South and Walleyes living in lakes grow larger than those in streams.

The gameness a fish shows depends also on the kind of tackle used. A quarter-pound Bluegill hauled in on a 20-pound test line puts up no fight at all, while the same fish caught on a limber fly rod and fine leader is a real battler.

Most fish, in fact, fight gamely when caught on light enough tackle. Light tackle puts more zest in a salt-water fish's fight, too, and really large-size battlers can be bested with light tackle if it is used properly. The fighting chance light tackle gives the fish makes fishing more fun.

Fish normally swim about as fast as a man walks. But when hooked, some fish literally burn the line from a reel. Marlin and sailfish may reach speeds of 60 miles an hour in short bursts. Tarpon can rip off line at 30 miles an hour, and even small game fish, including fresh-water trout and bass, have been clocked at 20 miles an hour. The harder and faster a fish fights the more exciting it is to catch, as any veteran fisherman will testify.

The principal sport fish of fresh and salt waters in North America are described and illustrated on the following pages. Included with the sport fish are some of the common rough and pest species that provide sport or fun simply because they are caught so abundantly or are good to eat.

Both the common and scientific names used in this book are those adopted and recommended by the American Fisheries Society.

Striped Bass

Tarpon

Croaker

11

# SALT-WATER FISHES

| WHERE AND WHEN | HOW AND WHY |

**TARPON** range over the coastal waters of the Gulf of Mexico and in the Atlantic north to Virginia and as far south as Brazil. Inshore fish, they often ascend rivers to fresh water. They are permanent residents in the Florida Keys and 10,000 Islands. In U.S. waters they are most abundant in spring and summer, migrating northward in spring.

Trolling, drifting, and still fishing are best methods for big Tarpon. Smaller fish are taken by spinning, bait casting, or fly fishing. Nocturnal feeders, they are caught most readily at night. Favored natural baits are live crabs, pinfish, pigfish, and mullet. Cut mullet or bonito are also good, as are jigs, plugs, spoons, and flies.

**BONEFISH** are found on the flats bordering warm seas the world over. In the continental U.S. they rarely occur north of Biscayne Bay on the Atlantic or the 10,000 Islands on the Gulf. They are plentiful the year round in the Florida Keys and the Bahamas. Most active on the rising tide, they feed night and day.

Baiting an area with conch chum, then still fishing is classic fishing method. More popular is stalking the fish by poling or wading across flats. Best natural baits are shrimp, hermit crabs, and conch. Effective lures are pork chunks, bucktail jigs, worm jigs, and flies. Spinning gear is best; fly tackle is more sporting.

**LADYFISH** are found in the inshore waters of tropical seas the world over. They are plentiful in the Gulf of Mexico and range northward in summer to the Carolinas in the Atlantic. Ladyfish are active all year in southern Florida, feeding day and night. They are caught around inlets and over deep flats.

Casting small bucktails with spinning tackle is the best way to catch Ladyfish. Best natural bait is live shrimp, but they also take cut mullet and live minnows. Streamer flies, small surface plugs, and spoons are good at times. Whatever the lure, it should be fished behind a heavy nylon or light wire leader.

**AMERICAN SHAD** enter rivers on the Atlantic from New England to North Florida. Hickory Shad do not occur abundantly south of the Carolinas. Both are caught in fresh water during spring spawning runs.

Most popular angling method is casting small spoons or brightly colored weighted flies with spinning tackle. Trolling is also practiced in slow rivers of the South. Shad are rarely taken on natural baits.

**TARPON**
*Megalops atlanticus*
Av., 5-20 lbs.
Common, 50-100 lbs.
Reaches, 300 lbs. plus

**BONEFISH**
*Albula vulpes*
Av., 3-4 lbs.
Common, 5-10 lbs.
Reaches, 20 lbs.

**LADYFISH**
*Elops saurus*
Av., ½-1 lb.
Common, 1-2 lbs.
Reaches, 7 lbs.

**AMERICAN SHAD**
*Alosa sapidissima*
Av., 2-4 lbs.
Common, 4-6 lbs.
Reaches, 10 lbs.

**HICKORY SHAD**
*Alosa mediocris*
Av., 1-2 lbs.
Common, 2-3 lbs.
Reaches, 4 lbs

13

| WHERE AND WHEN | HOW AND WHY |
|---|---|

**ATLANTIC MACKEREL** roam the open waters of the Atlantic north of Cape Hatteras. Schools appear off Hatteras in March, migrating northward to New England by late May, and there they venture into inside waters. Elsewhere, they stay offshore.

Trolling with feathers, spoons, or diamond jigs is the standard angling method. After a school is located by trolling, mackerel may be caught by casting with fly or spinning tackle. Natural baits are rarely used, but fish will hit trolled strip baits.

**KING MACKEREL** winter in the Caribbean and along the Florida Keys. In spring, migrations carry them into the northern Gulf and as far north as North Carolina. Usually found a mile or more offshore.

Trolling with spoons or large feathers is the most popular fishing method. Chumming with pieces of mullet is practiced in the western Gulf. Many are taken on trolled baits of ballyhoo or mullet when fishing for sailfish.

**SPANISH MACKEREL** range through inshore and offshore waters of the Gulf and the Atlantic south of Virginia capes. In summer they range northward; resident in southern Florida.

Trolling with small spoons or white bucktail and nylon jigs is the most popular method. Casting the same lures with spinning tackle also good. Minnows and shrimp are best natural baits.

**CERO MACKEREL** are rarely found in the U.S. north of the Florida Keys. Common in the Bahamas. They like coral reefs.

Ceros are best caught by trolling small bucktails or spoons around the outer reefs. Deep retrieves with bucktails are favored.

**PACIFIC (CHUB) MACKEREL** occur along Pacific Coast from Washington south to Mexico. Most abundant off beaches south of Santa Barbara to Ensenada.

Usually caught from piers or small boats on strip baits, live sardines, or anchovies. They readily strike trolled spoons, squids, and small bucktail jigs.

**PACIFIC SIERRA** range from Peru to Baja California. Rarely seen north of Ensenada.

Trolled strip baits, jigs, and spoons are effective. Good live baits are anchovies, sardines.

**WAHOO** are nowhere abundant, but are found in the Gulf Stream and over coral reefs south of Hatteras. Most numerous in Bahamas and West Indies.

Deep trolling over coral ledges is best method. Wire line is often used with large feathers or spoons. Best bait is whole Spanish Mackerel trolled deep.

### ATLANTIC MACKEREL
*Scomber scombrus*
Av., ½-1 lb.
Common, 1-2 lbs.
Reaches, 4 lbs.

### KING MACKEREL
*Scomberomorus cavalla*
Av., 6-10 lbs.
Common, 20-30 lbs.
Reaches, 75 lbs.

### SPANISH MACKEREL
*Scomberomorus maculatus*
Av., 1-2 lbs.
Common, 3-5 lbs.
Reaches, 12 lbs.

### CERO MACKEREL
*Scomberomorus regalis*
Av., 1-2 lbs.
Common, 4-6 lbs.
Reaches, 20 lbs.

### PACIFIC (CHUB) MACKEREL
*Scomber japonicus*
Av., 1 lb.
Common, 2-3 lbs.
Reaches, 6 lbs.

### PACIFIC SIERRA
*Scomberomorus sierra*
Av., 1-2 lbs.
Common, 3-5 lbs.
Reaches, 12 lbs.

### WAHOO
*Acanthocybium solanderi*
Av., 15-20 lbs.
Common, 30-40 lbs.
Reaches, 150 lbs.

15

**BONITOS** range from Long Island to Florida in the Atlantic and in the Gulf. In the Pacific they are found south of Pt. Conception. Usually stay offshore; most plentiful in summer.

Many Bonitos are caught by anglers trolling for Bluefish or for school tuna (10-100 lbs.). Strike strip baits, bucktails, spoons, and metal jigs. In Pacific, live sardines are favored.

**BLUEFIN TUNA** are found from Bahamas to Nova Scotia. In the Pacific they occur south of Pt. Conception offshore. Atlantic school tuna (10-100 lbs.) stay offshore, but giants (over 100 lbs.) work inshore in north.

School tuna are taken trolling with spoons, jigs, and plastic squids and fish. In Pacific, live sardines and anchovies are used. Giant tuna are chummed with herring and baited with mullet or mackerel.

**BLACKFIN TUNA** range south of Cape Hatteras to the Gulf of Mexico and the Caribbean. Bluewater fish, they roam open seas and edge of Gulf Stream. Summer fishing is best in U.S. waters.

Trolling with strip baits, bucktails, or spoons is best method. Large specimens often hit sailfish baits off Florida. Sometimes caught from compact schools by casting jigs, squids, or spoons.

**YELLOWFIN TUNA** roam the Atlantic south of Hatteras and the Pacific south of Santa Barbara. They are most plentiful in spring and summer in blue water well offshore.

Usually caught more by accident than design, these fish often strike trolled mullet or ballyhoo baits intended for sailfish or marlin. In Pacific waters, they pick up Bluefin Tuna baits.

**SKIPJACK TUNA** or "Oceanic Bonito" occur south of New Jersey in Atlantic and south to Pt. Conception in Pacific. Prefer blue water, summer weather.

Fast trolling with feathers, metal jigs, or spoons is most consistent method. Strip baits are fair for trolling. Live sardines are the favorite bait in the Pacific.

**LITTLE TUNNY** range from New Jersey south in the open sea and edge of the Gulf Stream. Sometimes come close to inlets and beaches. Summer and fall best.

Very fast trolling with strip baits, metal squids, or bucktail and feather jigs is best method. Casting the same lures works well when school is located.

**ALBACORE** are found in the Pacific north to Alaska, often in the deep blue water near shoal green. Most common in summer.

Caught from live-bait boats off California on anchovies and sardines. Trolling with feathers or metal jigs also good.

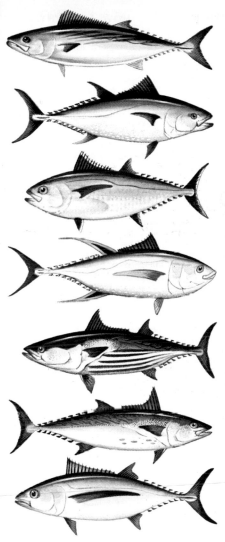

### ATLANTIC BONITO
*Sarda sarda*
Av., 3 lbs.
Common, 4-6 lbs.
Reaches, 15 lbs.

### BLUEFIN TUNA
*Thunnus thynnus*
school fish
Av., 15-25 lbs.
Common, 40-100 lbs.
giant fish
Av., 400 lbs.
Common, 60-700 lbs.
Reaches, 1500 lbs.

### BLACKFIN TUNA
*Thunnus atlanticus*
Av., 3-5 lbs.
Common, 7-10 lbs.
Reaches, 30 lbs.

### YELLOWFIN TUNA
*Thunnus albacares*
Av., 100 lbs.
Common, 150 lbs.
Reaches, 250 lbs.

### SKIPJACK TUNA
*Euthynnus pelamis*
Av., 6-10 lbs.
Common, 12-15 lbs.
Reaches, 40 lbs.

### LITTLE TUNNY
*Euthynnus alletteratus*
Av., 5-8 lbs.
Common, 10-12 lbs.
Reaches, 35 lbs.

### ALBACORE
*Thunnus alalunga*
Av., 10-15 lbs.
Common, 20 lbs.
Reaches, 80 lbs.

## WHERE AND WHEN

**SAILFISH** occur in the warmer waters of both the Atlantic and the Pacific. In the Atlantic, Sailfish range south of Hatteras, staying near the Gulf Stream, and into the Gulf of Mexico. In the Pacific, this magnificent blue-water fish is found throughout the tropical waters and north to Baja California. Sailfish are active the year round.

**MARLINS** roam the warm seas of the world. They are highly regarded game fish. The Blue Marlin occurs far out in the Gulf Stream from Cuba to Hatteras and also in the West Indies and Bahamas. Marlin fishing is best in spring and summer in U.S. and Bahamas waters. Striped Marlin range from the middle California coast south to Chile in deep, blue water. Active all year from Mexico south, they are found in California waters from spring until fall. White Marlin range from Montauk south to the West Indies. Most abundant late winter to summer in Florida and Bahamas; reach Long Island in late summer.

**SWORDFISH** are virtually world-wide in distribution, ranging south from Santa Cruz to the tropics and in the Atlantic from Nova Scotia to the Tropic of Capricorn. Best spots are the far offshore waters out of Montauk and Block Island; San Pedro to Avalon; and off Peru and Chile. Swordfish are highly prized and nowhere common.

## HOW AND WHY

Best method is trolling baits of mullet, ballyhoo, mackerel, or sardines, with line clipped to an outrigger. Sailfish strikes the skipping bait with his bill and jerks the line from the outrigger. As the line goes slack, the bait sinks as if stunned. Sailfish then picks up bait and runs with it. Slow trolling with live fish for bait is also a good method.

Trolling is by far the best method for marlins. Outriggers are used to keep the baits on the surface and to allow a dropback when a fish strikes. For Blue Marlin the tackle is heavy and the baits large—Bonefish, Spanish Mackerel, or Dolphin up to 5 or 6 pounds. For Striped Marlin the favored baits are mackerel, mullet, and flyingfish. These fish will also hit very large feather jigs and strip baits. White Marlin are caught on baits intended for sailfish. They also take trolled mackerel, eels, and squids. Plastic squid and small fish imitations make good lures, as do large feathers and nylon jigs.

Usual technique is to find the fish basking near the surface, then to troll baits of squid or mackerel in fish's line of vision. It is best to stop the boat and allow the bait to sink slowly in front of the fish. This brings many strikes. Tackle must be heavy, but drag on reel set light, as Swordfish have tender mouths despite power and stamina.

### SAILFISH
*Istiophorus albicans*

in the Atlantic:
Av., 30 lbs.
Common, 40-50 lbs.
Reaches, 120 lbs.

in the Pacific:
Av., 80-100 lbs.
Common, 150 lbs.
Reaches, 220 lbs.

### BLUE MARLIN
*Makaira nigricans*
Av., 300 lbs.
Common, 400-500 lbs.
Reaches, 800 lbs.

### STRIPED MARLIN
*Tetrapturus audax*
Av., 250 lbs.
Common, 400 lbs.
Reaches, 700 lbs.

### WHITE MARLIN
*Tetrapturus albidus*
Av., 50-60 lbs.
Common, 75 lbs.
Reaches, 160 lbs.

### SWORDFISH
*Xiphias gladius*
Av., 150 300 lbs.
Common, 400-700 lbs.
Reaches, 1200 lbs.

19

**GREATER AMBERJACK** ranges from Hatteras south to Brazil along edge of Gulf Stream, over offshore wrecks and around heavy coral reefs. Present all year in Florida and Bahamas. Migrate northward in summer.

Best method is slow drifting with live baits of grunts, croakers, or other small fish. Chum of fish chunks will excite fish to strike. Spoons and bucktails are good artificials. Hooked fish may be kept overboard to attract others.

**CREVALLE JACKS** range from North Carolina to the Caribbean. They are found the year round from Florida south; summer elsewhere. Enter bays and rivers, even fresh water in Fla.

Caught mostly by casting or trolling bucktail jigs, spoons, plugs, or flies. All natural baits are good, with live shrimp best. Crevalle Jacks are usually taken while seeking other fish.

**HORSE-EYE JACKS** are common in West Indies and Bahamas, also Fla. Range inshore and over offshore reefs.

Small spoons, jigs, and flies best fished with light tackle. Use fast retrieve. Night fishing is the most productive.

**BLUE RUNNERS** occur over same range as Crevalle but more in outside waters. Inlets good.

Best method is casting small bucktail jigs around buoys outside inlets. Spoons also good.

**BAR JACKS** range through the same waters as Yellow Jacks, often in the same schools.

Casting or trolling with small jigs, spoons, or strip baits are best methods. Use fast retrieve.

**YELLOW JACKS** are common from the Caribbean north to Florida Keys and Bahamas. They are found all year over reefs.

Fast trolling with metal jigs, spoons, or bucktails is best method. Same lures are also effective when cast.

**GREEN JACKS** range from Baja California to Peru. Most abundant off Central America.

Best caught trolling or casting with jigs, spoons, and squids. Live fishes, strip baits good.

**YELLOWTAILS** range from Point Conception southward to Guadalupe. They are most plentiful off Baja California and in the Gulf of California. Waters around islands with rocky shores, also kelp beds. All year Baja Calif., north in spring and summer.

Most popular method is chumming with live anchovies, butterfish or sardines, using same chum and bait. Slow trolling with feathers and spoons is also effective. Deep jigging with large bucktails or metal jigs can produce fine catches.

**GREATER AMBERJACK**
*Seriola dumerili*
Av., 10-20 lbs.
Common, 40-60 lbs.
Reaches, 150 lbs.

**CREVALLE JACK**
*Caranx hippos*
Av., 1-2 lbs.
Common, 8-12 lbs.
Reaches, 55 lbs.

**BLUE RUNNER**
*Caranx crysos*
Av., ½-1 lb.
Common, 2 lbs.
Reaches, 7 lbs.

**YELLOW JACK**
*Caranx bartholomaei*
Av., 1-2 lbs.
Common, 8-10 lbs.
Reaches, 15 lbs.

**GREEN JACK**
*Caranx caballus*
Av., ½-1 lb.
Common, 1-2 lbs.
Reaches, 5 lbs.

**YELLOWTAIL**
*Seriola lalandei*
Av., 10-15 lbs.
Common, 20-30 lbs.
Reaches, 90 lbs.

21

| WHERE AND WHEN | HOW AND WHY |
|---|---|

**FLORIDA POMPANO** occur along Atlantic Seaboard from Virginia to Florida and in Gulf of Mexico. A fish of surf, inlets, and bays; also offshore oil rigs in Gulf. Resident in Gulf and Florida, summer to the north.

Best method is surf fishing with baits of sand fleas or clam. Also good is casting and jigging with small bucktails and other jigs. Chumming with crushed clam or crab will attract Pompano to area to be fished.

**PERMIT,** or Giant Pompano, are found in limited numbers on the lower Gulf Coast of Florida, in the Florida Keys, and on east coast of Mexico. They like very deep passes, range over shallow flats also. Summer best.

Fishing deep in passes with blue crabs is best method. Permit can also be stalked on flats like Bonefish, using spinning tackle and bucktail lures. Pink jigs especially good. Crabs or live shrimp good baits for flats.

**AFRICAN POMPANO** range through the Caribbean and West Indies north to Florida Keys and Bahamas. Found over bright sand bottom near outer reefs. Fishing best from late winter through summer.

Trolling over reefs with strip baits, spoons, or metal jigs is best method. Troll fast up to 10 mph. Casting with either spinning or bait-casting gear and using spoons or bucktails is also a productive technique.

**LOOKDOWNS** occur in tropical Atlantic north to South Florida, sometimes straying farther north in summer. Common in Keys around bridges, inshore reefs or wrecks, and also in creeks. All year, nighttime best.

Caught by drifting live shrimp with tide; spinning and fly fishing are also good. Small streamer flies and bucktail jigs fished around bridge shadows at night catch many fish. Use very light tackle.

**BLUEFISH** are world-wide in distribution. They roam the western Atlantic from Maine to Brazil, including the Gulf of Mexico. Bluefish travel in schools, feeding well offshore, in the surf, around inlets, and into bays. Their migrations are erratic, but they prefer rather warm water. Found all year in Florida waters, roaming north to cooler waters from spring until fall.

Many methods are suitable for bluefishing. Offshore, trolling with metal squids or feathers is preferred. Near inlets and in bays, the fish are attracted by chumming with ground-up menhaden, then fished for by casting jigs or squids. In the surf they are caught by squidding (using artificial baits) or by fishing with cut mullet or menhaden. Will hit all lures, most baits.

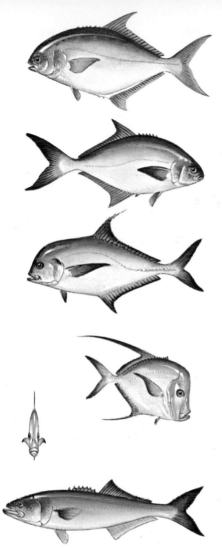

**FLORIDA POMPANO**
*Trachinotus carolinus*
Av., 1-2 lbs.
Common, 2-3 lbs.
Reaches, 7 lbs.

**PERMIT**
*Trachinotus falcatus*
Av., 15-20 lbs.
Common, 30 lbs.
Reaches, 50 lbs.

**AFRICAN POMPANO**
*Alectis ciliaris*
Av., 8-12 lbs.
Common, 20-30 lbs.
Reaches, 40 lbs.

**LOOKDOWN**
*Selene vomer*
Av., ½ lb.
Common, 1 lb.
Reaches, 3 lbs.

**BLUEFISH**
*Pomatomus saltatrix*
Av., 1-3 lbs.
Common, 5-10 lbs.
Reaches, 25 lbs.

23

| WHERE AND WHEN | HOW AND WHY |
|---|---|

**BLACK GROUPERS** range north to offshore South Carolina in summer but are resident in Florida waters and in the Gulf. They prefer coral reefs or other rocky bottom well offshore. Only the small fish venture close inshore. In Gulf best.

Deep trolling with feathers tipped with strip bait is best method. Drifting over rocks with baits of cut mullet, spiny lobster tail, or small live fish is also good. Do not use light tackle, for Black Grouper must be "horsed" from rocks.

**GAGS** are groupers that occur north into Florida and Bahamas waters and the Gulf of Mexico. They are found on coral reefs, but unlike Black Groupers, they also enter inshore and inside waters. Common in summer on inshore grass flats on Gulf Coast.

Spinning or bait casting with bucktails, spoons, or plugs are best methods. As Gags feed in comparatively shallow water, artificial lures can be used. Drifting over grass flats with live minnows or shrimp also good. Slow trolling best offshore.

**YELLOWFIN GROUPERS** are found in the Florida Keys, in the Bahamas, and on rocky bottom offshore in the Gulf. Small specimens move inshore in Keys around coral patches. Adult fish stay on rugged offshore reefs. Active all year.

Most Yellowfin Groupers are caught more or less by accident when fishing for other species. They strike bucktails, plugs, and spoons. Best baits are cut mullet, spiny lobster tail, and live shrimp. Bottom fishing on outer reefs best method.

**RED GROUPERS,** the most abundant groupers in U.S., range from the banks off North Carolina southward and into the Gulf of Mexico, where numerous. Found mostly on offshore banks but also come to inshore passes. Fishing good all year.

Still fishing and slow trolling with live fish or shrimp or with cut mullet are best methods. Feather, bucktail, and worm jigs worked deep are best lures. Red Groupers up to 3 or 4 pounds pursue lures actively; larger fish do not.

**NASSAU GROUPERS** are more numerous in the Bahamas than in U.S. waters, but they are fairly common in the Florida Keys. They occur south to the West Indies. They rarely venture far from coral reefs. Nassau Groupers are active all year.

Drifting over outer reefs with baits of live fish, cut mullet, or lobster tail fished near bottom is best method. Small specimens often strike bucktails and feathers intended for Yellowtail Snappers or other fish. A slow retrieve is best.

**BLACK GROUPER**
*Mycteroperca bonaci*
Av., 4-6 lbs.
Common, 10 lbs.
Reaches, 50 lbs.

**GAG**
*Mycteroperca microlepis*
Av., 1-2 lbs.
Common, 3-5 lbs.
Reaches, 20 lbs.

**YELLOWFIN GROUPER**
*Mycteroperca venenosa*
Av., 1-2 lbs.
Common, 4-5 lbs.
Reaches, 10 lbs.

**RED GROUPER**
*Epinephelus morio*
Av., 3-6 lbs.
Common, 8-10 lbs.
Reaches, 35 lbs.

**NASSAU GROUPER**
*Epinephelus striatus*
Av., 2-3 lbs.
Common, 5-10 lbs.
Reaches, 30 lbs.

25

| WHERE AND WHEN | HOW AND WHY |
|---|---|

**JEWFISH** are found in both inshore or offshore waters over reefs from the east coast of Florida to the Gulf Coast and Mexico. They often move into inside waters and passes. Active all year.

Still fishing with baits of live jacks or other fish is best method. Slack tide best time to fish. Tackle must be heavy to haul these powerful fish from their rocky underwater lairs.

**WARSAW GROUPER** are bottom fish of deep waters from the Carolinas to Gulf. Most plentiful spring and summer, offshore.

Usually caught on cut bait from drift boats bottom fishing on deep offshore reefs. Heavy tackle necessary.

**BLACK SEA BASS** are found in Atlantic from Cape Cod to Florida. A closely related species occurs in Gulf. Sea Bass are numerous offshore on hard bottom in depths to 100 feet. Smaller fish enter inside waters of Atlantic and Gulf. Fishing best in summer.

Bottom fishing from party boats accounts for most of the Sea Bass landed. Baits are usually clam or squid, but nearly any bait will do, as will any tackle, including hand lines. Deep jigging with bucktail jigs is good. Young fish in bays strike lures readily.

**GIANT SEA BASS** occur in the Pacific from middle California south to Mexico. Most abundant south of San Diego. They prefer deep channels and kelp beds, often close to shore. All year.

Best method is still fishing on bottom with baits of mullet, mackerel, or other fish, whole or cut. Tackle must be heavy, as for Spotted Jewfish. Use 80-pound test line, size 14/0 hook.

**KELP BASS** are found in the Pacific as far north as San Francisco. Most abundant south of Pt. Conception. Barred Sand Bass range north to Monterey. Both species are found in kelp beds all year. Summer fishing best.

Live-bait fishing with anchovies, queenfish, or tommy croakers best method. Strip baits, shrimp, and squid also good. Artificials effective if they can be used without hanging in kelp. Weedless spoons, bucktail jigs best.

**STRIPED BASS,** or Rockfish, range in the Atlantic from Maine to Florida, and in the Pacific from Coos Bay, Oregon to Monterey, California. A few fish live in rivers emptying into the northern Gulf. Stripers roam the surf, bays, and rivers. Spring and fall best, day or night.

Squidding with large plugs, jigs, rigged eels, and squids is popular when fish are in surf. Spinning with light tackle and lures good for river and bay fish. Fly fishing also good in bays. Trolling off beaches with plugs, feathers best for big fish. Squid, herring, crabs good natural baits.

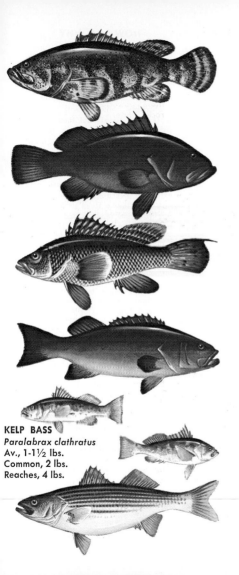

**JEWFISH**
*Epinephelus itajara*
Av., 25-50 lbs.
Common, 100-200 lbs.
Reaches, 700 lbs.

**WARSAW GROUPER**
*Epinephelus nigritus*
Av., 20-30 lbs.
Common, 100-200 lbs.
Reaches, 500 lbs.

**BLACK SEA BASS**
*Centropristes striatis*
Av., 1-1½ lbs.
Common, 2-3 lbs.
Reaches, 8 lbs.

**GIANT SEA BASS**
*Stereolepis gigas*
Av., 75-100 lbs.
Common, 200 lbs.
Reaches, 600 lbs.

**KELP BASS**
*Paralabrax clathratus*
Av., 1-1½ lbs.
Common, 2 lbs.
Reaches, 4 lbs.

**BARRED SAND BASS**
*Paralabrax nebulifer*
Av., 1-2 lbs.
Common, 3 lbs.
Reaches, 6 lbs.

**STRIPED BASS**
*Morone saxatilis*
Av., 5-10 lbs.
Common, 15-30 lbs.
Reaches, 70 lbs.

27

**SNAPPERS,** a family of tropical and subtropical fish of over 250 species, range in size from a few ounces to over 100 pounds. Gray Snappers, the most important species to sport fishermen, live on coral reefs and in creeks and bays. Active all year, they range north to Florida and the Gulf. Schoolmasters are found in same range and locations as Grays. Lane Snappers frequent grass flats and hard bottoms in same range. Muttonfish occur on reefs on both coasts of Florida. Yellowtails are abundant over reefs in Keys and Bahamas; Red Snappers in deep water (over 100 ft.) in Gulf and Atlantic from N.C. south.

All of the snappers (except Red Snapper) can be caught by the same methods. Chumming with chopped or ground-up mullet, preferably mixed with sand, works well to attract these wary fish. When the fish are taking chum freely, use unweighted baits of the chum on monofilament line. Bottom fishing with a bait of cut mullet is good, especially at night. Live shrimp are very effective in creeks and bays. Do not use either a float or a sinker. Bucktail and feather jigs are the best artificials and should be fished deep and retrieved jerkily. Red Snappers are caught bottom fishing with cut fish bait, usually from party boats.

**GRUNTS,** related to snappers, are a family of mostly tropical panfish. They feed day and night on bottom. The White Grunt occurs on Florida's lower east coast and in the Keys. Like most grunts it prefers hard bottom and is found both inshore and offshore. The Margate Grunt occurs in the Bahamas and Florida Keys. The Bluestriped Grunt ranges north to mid-Florida along both coasts. The French Grunt, a very small species, strays up Florida's east coast in summer. The Black Margate, largest of the grunts, is more abundant in Bahamas but also occurs in Keys. The Porkfish is found on Gulf and Atlantic coasts of south Florida. Pigfish occurs in Gulf and, in summer, north to Chesapeake Bay, where it is known as Hogfish.

Bottom fishing with light tackle is the best method in fishing for grunts. The best bait is live shrimp, though clam and cut mullet also work well. In the ideal rig, the line runs freely through an egg sinker, with a short monofilament leader and size 1/0 hook at the end. This allows biting fish to take out line without feeling the weight of the sinker. Use this rig in hard-bottomed swash channels, from bridges, and around coral heads. Tackle should be fresh-water style bait-casting or spinning gear. Most grunts will strike small artificial lures fished close to the bottom. Bluestriped Grunts, White Grunts, and Pigfish readily hit small jigs tipped with bits of shrimp or mullet. Fish the lures slowly, retrieving with short jerks.

### 1. GRAY SNAPPER
*Lutjanus griseus*
Av., ½-1 lb.
Common, 2-3 lbs.
Reaches, 20 lbs.

### 4. MUTTONFISH
*Lutjanus analis*
3-25 lbs.

### 2. SCHOOLMASTER
*Lutjanus apodus*
½-5 lbs.

### 5. YELLOWTAIL
*Ocyurus chrysurus*
½-7 lbs.

### 3. LANE SNAPPER
*Lutjanus synagris*
¼-3 lbs.

### 6. RED SNAPPER
*Lutjanus campechanus*
4-40 lbs.

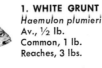

### 1. WHITE GRUNT
*Haemulon plumieri*
Av., ½ lb.
Common, 1 lb.
Reaches, 3 lbs.

### 4. FRENCH GRUNT
*Haemulon flavolineatum*
¼-1 lb.

### 2. MARGATE GRUNT
*Haemulon album*
½-8 lbs.

### 5. BLACK MARGATE
*Anisotremus surinamensis*
½-20 lbs.

### 3. BLUESTRIPED GRUNT
*Haemulon sciurus*
½-3 lbs.

### 6. PIGFISH
*Orthopristes chrysoptera*
¼-1½ lbs.

29

**PORGIES** of various species occur in the Atlantic from Cape Cod south to the West Indies. Sheepshead range from Chesapeake Bay to the Gulf Coast. Jolthead Porgies occur from southern Florida southward. Scup are found from Cape Cod to Hatteras, mostly offshore on hard bottoms. Southern Porgies, nearly identical in appearance to the more northern Scup, range from Hatteras to the Gulf over hard bottom. Grass Porgies are found in the Gulf on grass bottom, as are Pinfish, which occur in bays and lagoons from North Carolina to Texas.

Use light bait-casting or spinning gear for all porgies. The light-biting Sheepshead is best caught with the rig described for grunts (p. 28), using fiddler crabs or sandbugs for bait. Hang bait near piling just off bottom or over shell bed. At first sign of a tug, lower rod gently as fish pulls, then strike hard. Scup and Southern Porgies are caught by bottom fishing with baits of crab, clam, or shrimp. Jolthead Porgies are caught mostly by accident from party boats. Grass Porgies and Pinfish take live or cut shrimp fished over grassy bottom.

**BERMUDA CHUBS** are plentiful all year in Bermuda, Florida Keys, and Bahamas waters. They hover over coral heads, feed in the surf, and sometimes follow ships to feed on wastes thrown overboard.

Chubs are best caught on small baits of shrimp, crab, or cut fish. Use small hook (size 2–4) and fish near bottom. Strike hard to set hook in tough mouth. Bermuda Chubs strike flies and small jigs fished slowly.

**TRIPLETAILS** are known from Chesapeake Bay to Texas, but are common only from South Carolina south. Hang around buoys and pilings near inlets and passes. On Gulf Coast, enter inside water. All year southern Fla., to north summer.

Best method is spot casting to fish after sighting them at channel markers. Use medium-weight bait casting or spinning tackle and bucktail or feather jigs. Live crabs and shrimp are best natural baits. Pinfish are also good. Fish hit best on strong tide.

**SNOOK** are found in the inshore waters of the Atlantic and Gulf from Florida to Central America; also in Gulf of California and Pacific Coast of Mexico. Ascend rivers to fresh water, where they spend long periods. Feed day and night all year, but spring and summer best.

Bait casting, spinning, and fly fishing are all excellent methods. Snook strike nearly all artificial lures, including surface and underwater plugs, spoons, jigs, flies, and spinners. Cast lures close to shorelines where fish lie. Pinfish, mullet, and shrimp are good natural baits, used live.

## 1. SHEEPSHEAD
*Archosargus*
*probatocephalus*
Av., 1 lb.
Common, 3-5 lbs.
Reaches, 20 lbs.

## 2. JOLTHEAD PORGY
*Calamus bajonado*
1-8 lbs.

## 3. SCUP
*Stenotomus chrysops*
1-4 lbs.

## 4. GRASS PORGY
*Calamus arctifrons*
½-2 lbs.

## 5. PINFISH
*Lagodon rhomboides*
¼-1 lb.

## BERMUDA CHUB
*Kyphosus sectatrix*
Av., ½ lb.
Common, 1 lb.
Reaches, 4 lbs.

## TRIPLETAIL
*Lobotes surinamensis*
Av., 3-5 lbs.
Common, 8-10 lbs.
Reaches, 30 lbs.

## SNOOK
*Centropomus undecimalis*
Av., 2-4 lbs.
Common, 10-15 lbs.
Reaches, 65 lbs.

31

## WHERE AND WHEN

## HOW AND WHY

**WEAKFISH** range from Cape Cod to northern Florida in inshore waters. They are most abundant from Long Island to Virginia. Feeding day and night, they roam the surf and into bays and rivers. Summer best.

Use fresh-water bait casting, fly or spinning gear for both natural bait and artificial lure fishing. Good lures are bucktails, spoons, and streamers. Best baits are peeler crabs, squid, and shrimp. Night fishing best.

**SPOTTED SEATROUT** are common in the inshore waters of the Gulf and north in the Atlantic to Virginia, straying rarely to New Jersey in fall. Found in bays, inlets, and surf. Grass flats good. All year in South.

Spinning with small jigs and related lures is best method. Bait casting and fly fishing are also productive. Plugs and streamer flies good lures. Best natural baits are live shrimps and minnows, fished under a float.

**WHITE SEABASS,** closely related to Atlantic weakfishes, are found in the Pacific from Alaska to Baja California. Most abundant around kelp beds off southern California. Often enter inside waters. All year.

Best method is drifting over kelp beds and submerged banks with baits of live sardines or anchovies. Slow trolling with strip baits, spoons, or jigs also effective. Fish deep in daytime, near surface at night.

**ATLANTIC CROAKERS** occur from Delaware Bay to Texas, with the center of abundance Chesapeake Bay. Feed over shell or sand bottom in bays and lower reaches of rivers, and most active in late spring and summer.

Bottom fishing with baits of cut shrimp, clams, or peeler crabs is best method. It is preferable to drift slowly rather than to anchor. Bucktail and feather jigs will catch croakers when bumped slowly along bottom.

**SPOTFIN CROAKERS** are found in the Pacific from Pt. Conception to Pt. Banda. Feed in surf, bays, and sloughs and are active year round. Most abundant in late summer and fall.

Surf fishing with baits of mussel, clams, sandworms, or crabs is most popular method. Bottom fishing in bays with same baits is also good. Use fresh-water style tackle for most sport.

**YELLOWFIN CROAKERS** range from Pt. Conception to Gulf of California along sandy beaches and up to a mile offshore. Most abundant in Baja California. Late summer and fall.

Best method is surf fishing with baits of sea worms, clams, mussel, or crabs. Bottom fishing while slowly drifting with same baits is effective offshore. For most fun use very light tackle.

**WEAKFISH**
*Cynoscion regalis*
Av., 1 lb.
Common, 2-3 lbs.
Reaches, 15 lbs.

**SPOTTED SEATROUT**
*Cynoscion nebulosus*
Av., 1 lb.
Common, 3-5 lbs.
Reaches, 15 lbs.

**WHITE SEABASS**
*Atractoscion nobilis*
Av., 10-15 lbs.
Common, 20-30 lbs.
Reaches, 80 lbs.

**ATLANTIC CROAKER**
*Micropogonias undulatus*
Av., 1 lb.
Common, 2-3 lbs.
Reaches, 8 lbs.

**SPOTFIN CROAKER**
*Roncador stearnsi*
Av., 1 lb.
Common, 1½-2 lbs.
Reaches, 6 lbs.

**YELLOWFIN CROAKER**
*Umbrina roncador*
Av., ½ lb.
Common, 1 lb.
Reaches, 2 lbs.

33

**RED DRUM,** or Channel Bass, range along Atlantic and Gulf coasts from Delaware to Texas. They are surf and inlet dwellers in northern part of range (spring to fall) but prefer flats and shorelines in inside waters in Fla. and along Gulf all year.

Surf casting with crab, cut mullet, or Menhaden baits is classic method for large fish. Trolling off inlets with large spoons also good. Smaller fish, called "puppy drum," are taken on bucktail jigs or plugs with light tackle. Live shrimp and crab good.

**BLACK DRUM** are found in the inshore waters of the Atlantic from Delaware Bay to Florida, and over the Gulf Coast to Texas. Their favorite haunts are oyster bottoms in bays and lagoons. Spring and fall are best.

Still fishing with cut blue crab is best method. Fish on shell bottom where tide flow is strong. Other good baits are clam and shrimp. Surf tackle best for big fish, but fresh-water gear is fine for small fish.

**SILVER PERCH** are common from New Jersey to Texas in bays and lower reaches of rivers. All year in Florida.

Best method is bottom fishing with small baits or cut shrimp, crab, or mullet. Small jigs and squids are good fished deep.

**SPOTS** occur in bays and rivers from New Jersey to Texas. Especially abundant in Chesapeake Bay. Most active in summer.

Still fishing on bottom with small baits of shrimp, clam, or sea worms is best method. Use very light tackle; size 6 hooks.

**CALIFORNIA CORBINAS,** related to Atlantic whitings, are found inshore in the Pacific from Pt. Conception south to Gulf of California. Sandy surf best. Also bays on sand bottom in water 2 to 20 feet deep. All year.

Best method is surf fishing with baits of sea worms, crabs, clam, or shrimp. Bottom fishing in bays around old piers also good. Corbinas will strike small jigs and squids fished slowly along bottom. Use light tackle.

**KINGFISH** (Whitings) are represented by three species. Northern Kingfish range from Cape Cod to Virginia Capes; Southern Kingfish, from Maryland to Florida's east coast. Gulf Kingfish are common only on the Gulf Coast. All three species are fish of the surf and most active in summer.

Surf fishing with baits of sand bugs, shrimp, or crab is the best method. Where surf is light, use fresh-water tackle. In heavy surf or where long casts are needed, heavier squidding gear may be necessary. Whitings strike small jigs and squids bumped slowly along bottom.

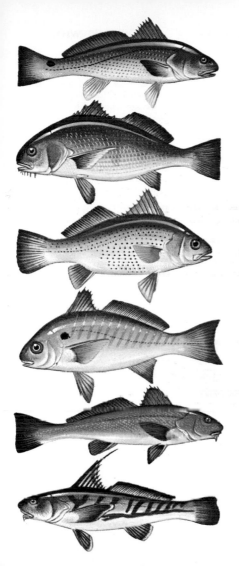

**RED DRUM**
*Sciaenops ocellatus*
Av., 5-10 lbs.
Common, 20-40 lbs.
Reaches, 80 lbs.

**BLACK DRUM**
*Pogonias cromis*
Av., 3-6 lbs.
Common, 30-50 lbs.
Reaches, 140 lbs.

**SILVER PERCH**
*Bairdiella chrysoura*
Av., ¼ lb.
Common, ½ lb.
Reaches, 1 lb.

**SPOT**
*Leiostomus xanthurus*
Av., ¼ lb.
Common, ½ lb.
Reaches, 1½ lbs.

**CALIFORNIA CORBINA**
*Menticirrhus undulatus*
Av., ½-1 lb.
Common, 1-2 lbs.
Reaches, 8 lbs.

**NORTHERN KINGFISH**
*Menticirrhus saxatilis*
Av., 1 lb.
Common, 1½-2 lbs.
Reaches, 3 lbs.

35

## WHERE AND WHEN

**TAUTOGS** range from Maine to South Carolina on rocky shores and around jetties, wrecks, and old pilings. Most plentiful from Cape Cod to Cape May, they bite best in spring and fall.

**CUNNERS** are found from Labrador to New Jersey inshore around docks, pilings, and jetties. Also offshore to depths of 200 feet. Often found with Tautogs. Spring to fall.

**CALIFORNIA SHEEPHEAD,** often called Sheepshead, occur from Monterey Bay to Gulf of California the year round. Fish around kelp beds, mussel beds, and rocky shores. Enter very shallow water on high tides.

**ROCKFISHES,** or Scorpionfishes, are an important family, with some 56 species on the Pacific Coast. The Bocaccio ranges from British Columbia to San Diego in water depths of 300 feet and over. The Olive Rockfish ranges from San Francisco to San Quentin Bay in shallow water, around kelp beds.

**SEAPERCHES and SURF-PERCHES** are important fish on the Pacific Coast. Seaperches generally occur in comparatively deep water or along rocky shores; surfperches are found off sandy beaches. Barred Surfperch roam California's sandy surfs south to San Diego all year. White Seaperch range from Vancouver to San Diego in bays and inlets the year round.

## HOW AND WHY

Still fishing on bottom with baits of green crab, fiddler crab, sea worms, grass shrimp, or clam is best method. Use medium-weight tackle, as these fish dive into rocks like groupers.

Bottom fishing with small baits of cut seaworms, clam, or lobster is best method. Use small hook (size 4 maximum) and fresh-water tackle to overcome their bait-stealing skill.

Best method is still fishing or slow drifting with baits of mussel, clam, shrimp, or crab. Ready biters. California Sheephead sometimes take live fishes or trolled strip baits or jigs. Deep fishing usually best.

Best method is still fishing with baits of live or dead fish, or mussel, clam, shrimp, or strip baits. Larger, deep-water species, like Bocaccio, prefer baits of small mackerel, herring, or other small fish. Rockfishes of shallow waters prefer mollusks or crustaceans, but will hit spoons and jigs slowly trolled.

Barred Surfperch and other surfperches are caught best by surf casting with baits of clam, mussel, rockworms, or sand crabs on small hooks. Fresh-water tackle is adequate, but heavier gear must be used sometimes to make long casts to reach fish. White Seaperch and other seaperches are caught by still fishing with small baits of sandworms, shrimp, mussel, or clam.

**CUNNER**
*Tautogolabrus adspersus*
Av., ¼ lb.
Common, ½-1 lb.
Reaches, 2 lbs.
▼

**TAUTOG**
*Tautoga onitis* ▲
Av., 1-4 lbs.
Common, 8-10 lbs.
Reaches, 20 lbs.

**CALIFORNIA SHEEPHEAD**
*Semicossyphus pulcher*
Av., 2-4 lbs.
Common, 5-10 lbs.
Reaches, 25 lbs.
◄

male

female

**OLIVE ROCKFISH**
*Sebastes serranoides*
Av., ½-1 lb.
Reaches, 3½ lbs.
▼

**BOCACCIO**
*Sebastes paucispinis*
Av., 2-3 lbs.
Common, 5-8 lbs.
Reaches, 18 lbs.
▲

**WHITE SEAPERCH**
*Phanerodon furcatus*
Av., ¼ lb.
Reaches, 1 lb.
▼

**BARRED SURFPERCH**
*Amphistichus argenteus*
Av., ½ lb.
Common, 1 lb.
Reaches, 2½ lbs.
▲

37

## WHERE AND WHEN

## HOW AND WHY

**POLLOCK** range from Nova Scotia to Long Island in open bays and offshore to depths of over 100 feet. Spring and fall best, but north of Cape Cod, Pollock are active all summer.

In offshore waters bottom fishing with baits of clam, squid, or herring is best method. Inshore, use spinning, bait casting, or fly fishing with bucktails, plugs, or streamer flies.

**ATLANTIC COD** occur in Atlantic south to Maryland. All year north of Cape Cod; winter south. Tomcods, smaller, enter bays from Nova Scotia to Va., fall to spring.

Best method for Atlantic Cod is bottom fishing offshore with baits of clam, squid, or herring. For Tomcod, still fishing with small baits of clam, seaworms best.

**HADDOCK** range from Nova Scotia to New Jersey in deep water (over 100 feet) offshore. Found all year on hard bottom.

Most practical method is hand-lining with heavy sinkers and baits of clam or squid. More a commercial than a sport fish.

**SILVER HAKES** range from Nova Scotia to New Jersey, coming inshore in fall and early winter. Active all summer in cold waters north of Cape Cod.

Best method is bottom fishing with baits of silverside minnows or sand launces. Strip baits, bucktails, and metal squids are effective if fished very deep.

**FLATFISHES** are important on both U.S. coasts. Summer Flounders occur from Cape Cod to Hatteras, inshore in summer. A southern form is found from Virginia to Texas. Winter Flounders, from Nova Scotia to Hatteras over mud flats in bays. Spring best. Starry Flounders occur all year from Alaska to Pt. Conception in inside waters. Calif. Halibut, from Pt. Conception to Mexico. Summer best.

Best method for Summer Flounders is drifting while dragging baits of live killifish along bottom. Deep-fished bucktails are good lures. Winter Flounders caught best by still fishing with seaworms, clams, or mussels. Chum of crushed mussels attracts fish. Starry Flounders taken by drifting bottom with strip baits or live minnows. California Halibut usually caught drifting with live fish or strip baits.

**WINTER FLOUNDER**
*Pseudopleuronectes americanus*
Av., ½-1½ lbs.
Common, 2-3 lbs.
Reaches, 5 lbs.

### POLLOCK
*Pollachius virens*
Av., 2-5 lbs.
Common, 5-10 lbs.
Reaches, 40 lbs.

### ATLANTIC COD
*Gadus morhua*
Av., 5-10 lbs.
Common, 20-25 lbs.
Reaches, 200 lbs.

### TOMCOD
*Microgadus tomcod*
Av., ¼ lb.
Common, ½ lb.
Reaches, 1 lb.

### HADDOCK
*Melanogrammus aeglefinus*
Av., 2-3 lbs.
Common, 4-6 lbs.
Reaches, 25 lbs.

### SILVER HAKE
*Merluccius bilinearis*
Av., ½-1 lb.
Common, 1-2 lbs.
Reaches, 6 lbs.

### STARRY FLOUNDER
*Platichthys stellatus*
Av., 1-3 lbs.
Common, 4-6 lbs.
Reaches, 20 lbs.

### CALIFORNIA HALIBUT
*Paralichthys californicus*
Av., 5-10 lbs.
Common, 15-30 lbs.
Reaches, 75 lbs.

**GREAT BARRACUDAS** roam inshore waters of Florida Keys and Bahamas; offshore, they range Gulf and north to Hatteras in Atlantic. Summer best.

Best method is trolling strip baits from small boats. Drifting with live fish baits and casting or trolling spoons, plugs, and bucktails are also good.

**PACIFIC BARRACUDAS** range from Pt. Conception to Baja California in offshore waters. All year off Baja California; spring to fall in Calif.

Drifting or still fishing with live sardines and anchovies or strip baits is best method. Feather jigs and metal squids often effective, either cast or trolled.

**DOLPHIN** range over the warm seas of the world in blue water. Plentiful in Gulf Stream from Hatteras south Fairly common off Baja California. Often near floating seaweed or debris. All year where water stays warm.

Best method is trolling with strip baits, bucktails, or spoons. Once school is located, keep a hooked fish in water and cast to school with jigs or plugs on light tackle. When fishing for large fish, use light trolling gear.

**COBIA** are found inshore and offshore in Gulf and on Atlantic seaboard north to Chesapeake Bay in summer. In winter, near edge of Gulf Stream off Florida Keys. They like shade of buoys, pilings, and lighthouses.

Still fishing with live crabs or small fish is best method. Float may be used to keep bait high, or bait may be drifted with tide on slack line. Spot casting to fish with large bucktails and feathers is exciting technique.

**LINGCOD** occur from Alaska to Pt. Conception, usually offshore in deep water. They enter shallow inshore water for spawning in winter months.

Best method in shallow water is slow trolling with strip baits or feather jigs. In deep water, bottom fishing with live fish, shrimp, or squid baits is best.

**HARDHEAD CATFISH** range from Virginia to Gulf of Mexico off beaches and in bays and rivers. Often in brackish water. All year in Fla.; summer elsewhere.

Bottom fishing with almost any natural bait is best method. Cut fish, shrimp preferred. Usually considered pests, Hardhead Catfish will hit deep-fished jigs.

**GAFFTOPSAIL CATFISH** are known from Hatteras to Florida in Atlantic, but are most abundant in Gulf. Commonly on sand bottom in surf and bays. Summer.

Best method is bottom fishing with cut mullet or shrimp. Slow drifting preferable to still fishing. Either bucktail or worm jigs are best artificials.

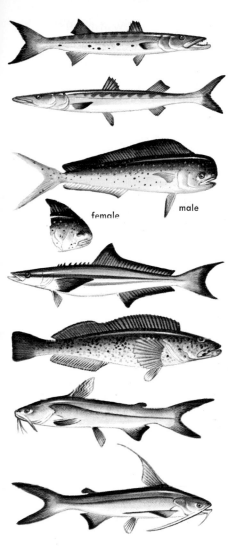

### GREAT BARRACUDA
*Sphyraena barracuda*
Av., 3-7 lbs.
Common, 10-20 lbs.
Reaches, 70 lbs.

### PACIFIC BARRACUDA
*Sphyraena argentea*
Av., 2-3 lbs.
Common, 4-6 lbs.
Reaches, 12 lbs.

### DOLPHIN
*Coryphaena hippurus*
Av., 2-4 lbs.
Common, 10-15 lbs.
Reaches, 75 lbs.

female    male

### COBIA
*Rachycentron canadum*
Av., 8-10 lbs.
Common, 20-30 lbs.
Reaches, 100 lbs.

### LINGCOD
*Ophiodon olongatus*
Av., 8-12 lbs.
Common, 15-20 lbs.
Reaches, 70 lbs.

### HARDHEAD CATFISH
*Arius felis*
Av., ½-1 lb.
Common, 1-1½ lbs.
Reaches, 3 lbs.

### GAFFTOPSAIL CATFISH
*Bagre marinus*
Av., 1-2 lbs.
Common, 2-3 lbs.
Reaches, 8 lbs.

41

| WHERE AND WHEN | HOW AND WHY |
|---|---|

**ATLANTIC SPADEFISH** range from Chesapeake Bay to Texas, south through Caribbean. Primarily coral reef fish; also like oyster bottoms, pilings, wrecks. Abundant near oil rigs in Gulf. All year from Fla. south.

Best method is still fishing with small baits of clam, shrimp, or crab. Use rig and technique that have been described for grunts (page 28). Atlantic Spadefish fight hard, but fresh-water tackle is adequate.

**QUEEN TRIGGERFISH** occur in Florida and on Gulf Coast, north to Hatteras in summer. On coral reefs and around wrecks and pilings. All year in Florida and southern Gulf.

Still fishing or drifting with baits of fiddler crab, shrimp, or cut fish is best method. Fish are usually but not always near bottom. Small bucktails are effective artificials.

**PORCUPINE FISH** are found from Florida and Bahamas south to West Indies over coral reefs and hard bottom. All year.

Still fishing or slow drifting with deep-fished baits of shrimp, spiny lobster pieces, or cut fish is best method.

**PUFFERS** range from Cape Cod to Texas, the northern form being found south to Florida, where southern form takes over. Grassy bays, shell bottoms.

Best method is still fishing or slow drifting with small hooks and baits of cut shrimp or crab. Voracious though small-mouthed, Puffers strike bucktails readily.

**OYSTER TOADFISH** are found in bays and rivers from New Jersey to Gulf, south to Caribbean. Summer north of Florida.

Bottom fishing with any natural bait is effective in catching this nuisance fish. Jigs are fairly good artificials.

**BIGHEAD SEAROBINS** occur over Gulf Coast and north in Atlantic to Hatteras. Carolina Searobins range north to N.J.

Best method is bottom fishing with baits of crab or shrimp. Bottom-bumped bucktails and feathers are good artificials.

**HOUNDFISH** range through the Caribbean and north to Bahamas and southern Fla. All year over shallow offshore banks.

Casting with strip baits or small bucktails is best method. Use spinning tackle, small hooks, and light, braided wire leaders.

**ATLANTIC NEEDLEFISH** are common off Florida, straying north to New Jersey in summer. Near surface, inshore.

Fly fishing with small streamers is best method. Fish also hit small spinning bucktails, pork rinds, and strip baits.

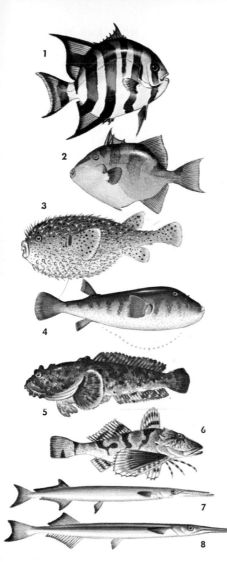

### 1. ATLANTIC SPADEFISH
*Chaetodipterus faber*
Av., 1 lb.
Common, 2-3 lbs.
Reaches, 15 lbs.

### 2. QUEEN TRIGGERFISH
*Balistes vetula*
Av., ½-1 lb.
Common, 1-1½ lbs.
Reaches, 3 lbs.

### 3. PORCUPINE FISH
*Diodon hystrix*
Av., 1-2 lbs.
Common, 3-5 lbs.
Reaches, 20 lbs.

### 4 NORTHERN PUFFER
*Sphoeroides maculatus*
Av., ¼ lb.
Common, ½ lb.
Reaches, 1 lb.

### 5. OYSTER TOADFISH
*Opsanus tau*
Av., ¼-½ lb.
Common, 1 lb.
Reaches, 2 lbs.

### 6. BIGHEAD SEAROBIN
*Prionotus tribulus*
Av., ¼-½ lb.
Common, 1 lb.
Reaches, 2½ lbs.

### 7. HOUNDFISH
*Tylosurus crocodilus*
Av., 1 lb.; 2 feet
Common, 2-3 lbs; 3-4 feet
Reaches, 10 lbs.; 5 feet

### 8. ATLANTIC NEEDLEFISH
*Strongylura marina*
Av., ¼ lb.; 15 in.
Common, ½ lb.; 1½ feet
Reaches, 3 lbs.; 4 feet

43

**SHORTFIN MAKO SHARKS** range over warm, deep waters of Atlantic and Pacific but are nowhere abundant. Most common around New Zealand. Frequently seen in Gulf Stream, sometimes near schools of King Mackerel, on which they prey.

Best method is trolling baits of whole rigged fish such as mackerel or mullet with fairly heavy tackle (80- to 130-pound test line). Usually caught by accident when trolling for tuna, marlin, or swordfish. Basking Makos occasionally take baits.

**HAMMERHEAD SHARKS** (five species) are found in the Atlantic and the Pacific. Very common in large passes along Gulf Coast. Often attack hooked Tarpon. All year in South.

Best method is still fishing on bottom with large baits of cut fish and heavy tackle. Bloody or oily fish like bonito or tuna make best baits. Night fishing most productive.

**TIGER SHARKS,** always very dangerous, range inshore and offshore in all warm seas. Very common off Florida and Gulf Coast, especially in the Gulf Stream. Active all year.

Best method is drifting in or near Gulf Stream with large, unweighted cut baits of bonito, tuna, or other bloody fish. Use 130-pound test line, chain leader, 16/0 hook, 12/0 reel.

**SAND TIGERS** are found on the Atlantic seaboard from New Jersey and south to Brazil. All year in South.

Still fishing at night on fairly shallow flats with baits of cut fish is best method. Tackle may be relatively light.

**DOGFISH** are common in the Atlantic. Spiny Dogfish occur inshore from Nova Scotia to North Carolina. Smooth Dogfish range south to Florida.

Bottom fishing in summer with baits of crab, shrimp, or squid is a sure way to hook these nuisances. They are major pests on the middle Atlantic seaboard.

**STING RAYS** are common over the entire Atlantic seaboard south of Cape Cod. The southern form ranges north to Hatteras; the northern form to Cape Cod.

Pests rather than gamefish, Sting Rays may be caught at any time when bottom fishing. Best baits are clam, crab, or shrimp, but cut fish will also catch them.

**SKATES** of various species are found in the Atlantic from Nova Scotia to Florida, but most occur only north of Hatteras. Inshore in surf and bays.

Very easily caught by bottom fishing with almost any bait. Skates are considered pests rather than gamefish. Surf fishing is probably the best method.

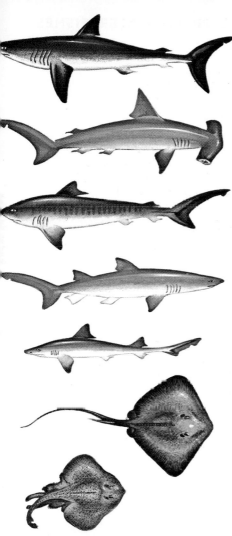

### SHORTFIN MAKO SHARK
*Isurus oxyrinchus*
Av., 100-150 lbs.
Common, 300-500 lbs.
Reaches, 1,000 lbs.; 12 ft.

### SMOOTH HAMMERHEAD
*Sphyrna zygaena*
Av., 100-150 lbs.
Common, 300-600 lbs.
Reaches, 1,400 lbs.; 13 ft.

### TIGER SHARK
*Galeocerdo cuvieri*
Av., 400-600 lbs.
Common, 900-1,500 lbs.
Reaches, 2,000 lbs.; 18 ft.

### SAND TIGER
*Odontaspis taurus*
Av., 30-50 lbs.
Common, 100 lbs.
Reaches, 400 lbs.; 10 ft.

### SMOOTH DOGFISH
*Mustelus canis*
Av., 4-7 lbs.
Common, 10-12 lbs.
Reaches, 30 lbs.

### SOUTHERN STINGRAY
*Dasyatis americana*
Av., 10-20 lbs.
Common, 35 lbs.
Reaches, 100 lbs.

### LITTLE SKATE
*Raja erinacea*
Av., 3-4 lbs.
Common, 8 lbs.
Reaches, 15 lbs.

# SALT- AND FRESH-WATER FISHES

| WHERE AND WHEN | HOW AND WHY |
|---|---|

**CHINOOK (KING) SALMON** are found in bays and rivers from Monterey to Alaska, also stocked and thriving in Great Lakes. Spawning runs in summer and fall.

Best method in salt-water bays is deep trolling with spoons or spinners. Drifting with live baits also effective. Sometimes taken on small spinners in fresh water.

**CHUM SALMON** range along the Pacific Coast from northern California to Alaska, ascending rivers short distances to spawn. Summer and early fall best.

Trolling with spoons or spinners accounts for a few Chum Salmon, but these fish are not easily caught. Still fishing in bays with baits of crabmeat best.

**SOCKEYE SALMON** occur on the Pacific Coast from northern California to Aleutian Islands. Common about islands and in swift tideways. Enters fresh water to spawn in summer.

Slow, deep trolling in tideways with spoons, jigs, or strip baits is good method. Best is "mooching," a technique of trolling a strip bait upward from bottom at about $45°$ angle (p. 123).

**COHO SALMON** range from northern California to Alaska in bays and river mouths. Like other salmons, enter fresh water to spawn. Runs occur in late summer prior to fall spawning.

Best technique is casting a weighted strip bait, allowing to sink, then retrieving upward at an angle. Slow trolling with spoons fair. Fly fishing effective in fresh water.

**HUMPBACK SALMON** are found on the Pacific Coast from northern California to northwestern Alaska. Spawning runs in September and October.

Best method is slow trolling with strip baits, crawfish tails, or brightly colored jigs. Small flashy spinning lures are effective just before spawning runs.

**ATLANTIC SALMON** ascend the cold, pure rivers on Atlantic Coast from Maine north through the Maritime Provinces. Also in northwestern Europe. Spring to early fall best.

Only method is highly specialized fly fishing. Since fish do not feed on spawning runs, flies are designed to appeal to their curiosity or arouse their anger. Elaborate fly patterns are used.

**LANDLOCKED SALMON,** a form of Atlantic Salmon, are found in cold lakes and streams from New York to Canada and Labrador. Spring and fall best.

Best method is trolling with streamer flies, spoons, or spinners. In midsummer, deep trolling is necessary to reach fish. Fly casting effective in spring.

### CHINOOK (KING) SALMON
*Oncorhynchus tshawytscha*
Av., 10-15 lbs.
Common, 20-30 lbs.
Reaches, 100 lbs.

### CHUM SALMON
*Oncorhynchus keta*
Av., 6-8 lbs.
Common, 10-15 lbs.
Reaches, 30 lbs.

### SOCKEYE SALMON
*Oncorhynchus nerka*
Av., 3-5 lbs.
Common, 10 lbs.
Reaches, 15 lbs.

### HUMPBACK SALMON
*Oncorhynchus gorbuscha*
Av., 3-4 lbs.
Common, 5-6 lbs.
Reaches, 10 lbs.

### COHO SALMON
*Oncorhynchus kisutch*
Av., 5-10 lbs.
Common, 12-15 lbs.
Reaches, 30 lbs.

### ATLANTIC SALMON
*Salmo salar*
Av., 10-12 lbs.
Common, 15-25 lbs.
Reaches, 60 lbs.

### LANDLOCKED SALMON
*Salmo salar*
Av., 2-4 lbs.
Common, 6-8 lbs.
Reaches, 20 lbs.

47

# FRESH-WATER FISHES

## WHERE AND WHEN

## HOW AND WHY

**BROOK TROUT,** originally native to northeastern U.S. and eastern Canada, have been introduced into streams and ponds over northern half of country. Most active spring and fall.

Fly casting with wet flies, dry flies, or streamers is most popular method. Best in early spring is bait fishing with worms or small minnows. Large Brook Trout strike spoons, small plugs.

**BROWN TROUT,** introduced to North America from Europe, occur in cool lakes and streams coast to coast but can tolerate warmer water than Brook Trout.

Best method is dry-fly fishing, for these trout are active surface feeders. Wet flies, streamers also good. Worms and minnows best baits in early spring.

**GOLDEN TROUT** are found in the High Sierras at altitudes of 10,000 feet and over. Once native to California, they like cold, deep lakes. Summer best.

Best method is fly casting with wet flies, streamers, and small spinners. Dry flies are good in late summer. Best natural baits are small minnows.

**CUTTHROAT TROUT** range from the Rocky Mountains west to the Pacific from Alaska to California. Found in lakes and streams, often enter salt water.

In streams, wet- or dry-fly fishing is best. In lakes, bait casting, spinning, or trolling with spoons, spinners, or plugs is effective. Small minnows good.

**DOLLY VARDEN TROUT** are found in coastal streams from northern California to northwestern Alaska. Migrate seaward in spring, inland in fall.

Best methods are bait casting or spinning with spoons or spinners. Wet flies and streamers good for small fish. Best baits are small, live fishes.

**RAINBOW TROUT,** native to western North America, have been introduced into cold lakes and streams over much of U.S. Enter salt water on Pacific Coast. Spring and summer.

Best method for streams is fly casting with wet or dry flies and streamers. Bait fishing with worms and salmon eggs also good. Trolling with spoons or spinners best in lakes.

**LAKE TROUT** are found in cold, deep lakes of northern U.S. and Canada. In summer they go deep (often to 100 ft. or more) to cold water (45°F.). Feed in shallows spring and fall.

Usual method is deep trolling, using spoons and wire line. In early spring and fall fly fishing, bait casting, and spinning are feasible. Caught through ice with live or cut fish baits.

### BROOK TROUT
*Salvelinus fontinalis*
Av., ¼-½ lb.
Common, 1-2 lbs.
Reaches, 10 lbs.

### BROWN TROUT
*Salmo trutta*
Av., ½-1½ lbs.
Common, 2-4 lbs.
Reaches, 30 lbs.

### GOLDEN TROUT
*Salmo aguabonita*
Av., ½ lb.
Common, 1 lb.
Reaches, 10 lbs.

### CUTTHROAT TROUT
*Salmo clarki*
Av., ½-1½ lbs.
Common, 2-3 lbs.
Reaches, 40 lbs.

### DOLLY VARDEN TROUT
*Salvelinus malma*
Av., 5-7 lbs.
Common, 10-15 lbs.
Reaches, 30 lbs.

### RAINBOW TROUT
*Salmo gairdneri*
Av., ½-2 lbs.
Common, 4-8 lbs.
Reaches, 35 lbs.

### LAKE TROUT
*Salvelinus namaycush*
Av., 5-10 lbs.
Common, 15-20 lbs.
Reaches, 60 lbs.

**LARGEMOUTH BASS** are found in lakes, streams, and rivers in the U.S., Canada, and Mexico. Slow streams and weedy lakes are best. Sometimes enter brackish water. Most active at dawn and dusk — all year in South, summer to fall in North.

Bait casting, fly fishing, and spinning with many types of plugs, spoons, spinners, flies, popping bugs, pork rinds, and plastic earthworms. Weedless lures needed for weedy shallows. Best natural baits are live shiners, grasshoppers, and frogs.

**SMALLMOUTH BASS** prefer clear, cool rivers, streams, and lakes. Found from Canada to southern U.S., except in Gulf states. Most active early summer and fall; feed day and night.

In streams, best methods are fly fishing and spinning with spinner flies or bucktails; also bait fishing with live hellgrammites, minnows, worms. In lakes, bait casting or spinning with plugs.

**SPOTTED BASS**, found from Ohio and West Virginia to eastern Texas, prefer deep pools and slow streams in North, favor clear fast streams in southern range. Fishing best in fall.

Fly fishing with small surface bugs, spinner flies, or streamers recommended. Spinning with small plugs and spoons also good. Best natural baits are earthworms, crayfish, minnows.

**SUNFISH** are common. Principal species is Bluegill, found in every state. Bluegills, Pumpkinseeds, and Longears prefer lakes and ponds but also occur in streams. Rock Bass are found in rocky streams and cool lakes. Warmouths like sluggish creeks. Spotted Sunfish and Redears prefer warm cypress lakes. Redbreasts like clear streams.

Best method for most sunfish is still fishing with baits of worms, insects, or crayfish. Use a light cane pole, monofilament line, and small hook. A bobber to hold the bait off bottom and to signal bites adds to the fun. Fly fishing with wet flies, dry flies, or small popping bugs is excellent. Ice fishing is also productive for taking Bluegills.

**CRAPPIES** have been widely introduced into waters over much of the U.S. Black Crappies like clear water; White Crappies tolerate silt. Spring and fall best.

Try still fishing or slow trolling with small live minnows. Fly casting and spinning with streamers, spoons, spinners or jigs are also good methods.

**BLACK CRAPPIE**
*Pomoxis nigromaculatus*
Av., $\frac{1}{2}$ lb.
Common, 1 lb.
Reaches, 3 lbs.

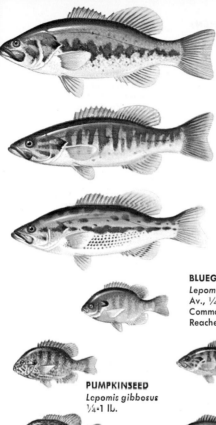

**LARGEMOUTH BASS**
*Micropterus salmoides*
Av., 1-2½ lbs.
Common, 4-7 lbs.
Reaches, 18 lbs.

**SMALLMOUTH BASS**
*Micropterus dolomieui*
Av., 1 lb.
Common, 2-4 lbs.
Reaches, 10 lbs.

**SPOTTED BASS**
*Micropterus punctulatus*
Av., ½ lb.
Common, 1 lb.
Reaches, 2 lbs.

**BLUEGILL**
*Lepomis macrochirus*
Av., ¼-½ lb.
Common, ¾-1 lb.
Reaches, 3 lbs.

**PUMPKINSEED**
*Lepomis gibbosus*
¼-1 lb.

**WARMOUTH**
*Lepomis gulosus*
¼-1½ lbs.

**LONGEAR SUNFISH**
*Lepomis megalotis*
¼-1 lb.

**SPOTTED SUNFISH**
*Lepomis punctatus*
⅛-½ lb.

**ROCK BASS**
*Ambloplites ariommus*
¼-2 lbs.

**REDBREAST SUNFISH**
*Lepomis auritus*
¼-1 lb.

| WHERE AND WHEN | HOW AND WHY |
|---|---|

**WHITE BASS** are found in lakes and streams in Canada and the Great Lakes region, south through the Mississippi Valley to eastern Texas. Schools often feed at surface. Spring and summer best.

In spring, still fishing with live minnows or worms is best. In summer, when White Bass are in schools and feeding at surface, try spinning, bait casting, and fly fishing with spoons, spinners, or streamer flies.

**YELLOW BASS** live in rivers, lakes, and streams through the Mississippi Valley to the Gulf Coast. Most abundant in southern areas. Usually form large schools in spring and summer.

Still fishing with live minnows or small crayfish is probably best. Spinning and fly fishing with small spoons, spinners, and streamer flies are also good methods, as for White Bass.

**WHITE PERCH** occur in streams or brackish rivers and bays from Maine to South Carolina. Common in fresh-water lakes in New England, where they bite well all summer. Most active in spring and fall in Chesapeake Bay and tributaries.

Best method is slow trolling with minnow and spinner combinations. After a school is located, still fishing with live minnows or grass shrimps is best. Also try fly fishing with spinner flies or tiny spoons, and spinning with small jigs or spoons.

**YELLOW PERCH** are found in most fresh waters along the Atlantic seaboard south to the Carolinas, in the Great Lakes region and Mississippi Valley. Prefer lakes, but live in tidal rivers, creeks, and lazy inland streams. Active all year.

Still fishing with live minnows works well, winter or summer. Fly fishing with streamers, spinner flies, or spoons is very effective in spring and fall. Spinning with small spoons or jigs is equally good. Jigging spoons are effective for ice fishing.

**WALLEYES,** native to the Great Lakes and rivers of northeastern U.S., have been introduced into clear rivers and firm-bottomed, cool lakes across the country. They are night feeders, most active in spring and fall.

Trolling at night with June bug spinner trailing a night crawler, eel, or minnow is best. Still fishing with live minnows is also good. Also effective are bait casting or spinning with deep-running plugs, spoons, or jigs.

**SAUGERS** are common in lower Great Lakes, TVA lakes, and western Appalachian rivers. Spring and fall are best.

Best method is slow, deep trolling with June bug spinner and minnow combinations. Still fishing with minnows is also good.

**WHITE BASS**
*Morone chrysops*
Av., 1 lb.
Common, 1½-2 lbs.
Reaches, 5 lbs.

**YELLOW BASS**
*Morone mississippiensis*
Av., ½ lb.
Common, 1-1¼ lbs.
Reaches, 3 lbs.

**WHITE PERCH**
*Morone americanus*
Av., ½ lb.
Common, 1 lb.
Reaches, 4 lbs.

**YELLOW PERCH**
*Perca flavescens*
Av., ½ lb.
Common, 1-1¼ lbs.
Reaches, 3 lbs.

**WALLEYE**
*Stizostedion vitreum*
Av., 2-4 lbs.
Common, 7-10 lbs.
Reaches, 20 lbs.

**SAUGER**
*Stizostedion canadense*
Av., ½ lb.
Common, 1 lb.
Reaches, 2 lbs.

53

| WHERE AND WHEN | HOW AND WHY |
|---|---|

**NORTHERN PIKE** live in shallow weedy areas in lakes and rivers in Canada and northern U.S. west through Great Lakes. Bite all year; spring, fall best.

Best method is bait casting with wobbler spoons or spinner-bucktail combinations. Plugs also good. Live suckers and small perch are best baits.

**MUSKELLUNGE** occur in Canada and in northern U.S. from New York to Great Lakes area. Also in streams on west side of Appalachians. Prefer weed beds in shallows of lakes and rivers.

Bait casting and trolling with large spoons, plugs, and spinner lures are best methods. Repeated casting to likely spots is advisable. Still fishing with live chubs or suckers is also good.

**CHAIN PICKEREL** are common in weedy lakes and quiet streams from Maine to Fla. and throughout Mississippi Valley.

Bait casting and spinning with wobbling spoons or spinner lures are preferred. Still fishing with live minnows also good.

**NORTHERN SQUAWFISH** are found in Pacific Coast rivers from central Calif. northward. Abundant in Owyhee Reservoir, Ore.

Best method is fly fishing with wet flies, dry flies, or streamers. Spinning or bait casting with plugs and spoons also effective.

**CREEK CHUBS** occur in small clear streams from Canada to Georgia and west to the Ozarks.

Fly fishing with small wet or dry flies and still fishing with worms are good methods.

**FALLFISH** range from Maritime Provinces to Va., in streams.

Best method is fly fishing with small wet flies and streamers.

**ARCTIC GRAYLINGS** are found in Alaska and British Columbia, in streams tributary to Arctic Ocean. Subspecies found in Montana's Madison and Gallatin rivers. Caught any time streams are ice free.

Best method is fly fishing. Wet flies of standard trout patterns are good, but they should be fished deep. Graylings take a fly very gently, and you must be alert to hook them. During fly hatches, dry flies may work well.

**SHEE-FISH** are common in most large streams and some lakes (Great Slave and Great Bear) in Arctic Canada. Often enter salt water. Shee-fish are active year round and may be taken whenever water is ice free.

Best methods are bait casting and spinning with fairly large plugs, spoons, or spinners. Still fishing with baits of live suckers or other small fish (to 12 in. long) also works well. Trolling good near river mouths.

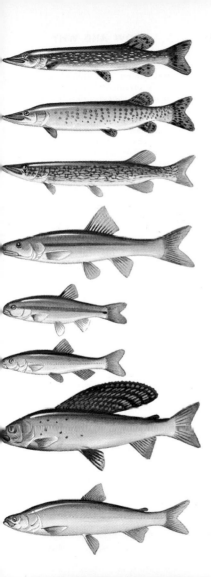

### NORTHERN PIKE
*Esox lucius*
Av., 4-5 lbs.
Common, 10-15 lbs.
Reaches, 45 lbs.

### MUSKELLUNGE
*Esox masquinongy*
Av., 8-10 lbs.
Common, 15-25 lbs.
Reaches, 70 lbs.

### CHAIN PICKEREL
*Esox niger*
Av., 1-1½ lbs.
Common, 2-3 lbs.
Reaches, 10 lbs.

### NORTHERN SQUAWFISH
*Ptychocheilus oregonensis*
Av., 2-4 lbs.
Common, 10-15 lbs.
Reaches, 60 lbs.

### CREEK CHUB
*Semotilus atromaculatus*
¼-1 lb.

### FALLFISH
*Semotilus corporalis*
¼-3 lbs.

### ARCTIC GRAYLING
*Thymallus arcticus*
Av., 1 lb.
Common, 2 lbs.
Reaches, 3 lbs.

### SHEE-FISH
*Stenodus leucichthys*
Av., 5-10 lbs.
Common, 20-30 lbs.
Reaches, 50 lbs.

## WHERE AND WHEN

## HOW AND WHY

**CATFISH,** native to much of the U.S. east of the Rockies, have been established in the West. Channel Catfish are common in clear rivers on Atlantic seaboard and in Mississippi Valley. Flathead Catfish occur in slow rivers from the Great Lakes through the Mississippi Valley and are most abundant in the South. Blue Catfish are found in the Mississippi and its tributaries, also in other slow rivers and mud-bottomed lakes of Southeast. White Catfish occur in rivers from New York to Florida and have been introduced successfully in California waters.

Most catfish are caught by bottom fishing with natural or specially prepared baits. Stink baits made of cheese, dried blood, or spoiled chicken entrails are favorites. Night fishing is generally best. Channel Catfish feed more by sight and less by scent than other catfish and often bite well in daytime. They strike such artificial lures as spoons, jigs, and spinner flies. Flathead Catfish prefer stink baits, cut fish, or crayfish tails. Blue Catfish will bite cut or whole fish as well as stink baits. White Catfish can be caught on worms, minnows, or crayfish.

**BULLHEADS** are popular over much of the U.S. Brown Bullheads occur in lakes and streams from Maine to Fla.; also in Great Lakes region, Ohio Valley, and Calif. Black Bullheads found from Hudson Bay south to Gulf Coast. Yellow Bullheads common from northern Midwest to Atlantic coast, south to Fla.

Bottom fishing at night is the best method for all bullheads. They also bite well during daylight hours in roiled waters. Baits may be cheese, stink baits, or even soap. The more conventional worms, doughballs, crayfish, or minnows will also catch bullheads. Worms are probably used the most.

**CARP and SUCKERS** provide sport for many anglers. Carp are found in lakes and streams of all U.S. mainland states except Maine and Florida. Suckers occur in clear streams east of Rockies. Spring best.

Best method for Carp is still fishing on bottom with doughballs or special preparations which may be purchased in cans. Do not use sinker or float. For suckers, still fish on bottom with worms. Night fishing best.

**BOWFINS, GARS, and OTHER ROUGHFISH** are found in most rivers, streams, lakes, and canals. Few furnish sport.

Most roughfish are caught while seeking game species. Bowfins, gars, and sturgeons may be caught with cut baits.

**BOWFIN**
*Amia calva*
2-20 lbs.

### CHANNEL CATFISH
*Ictalurus punctatus*
Av., 2-3 lbs.
Common, 6-8 lbs.
Reaches, 55 lbs.

### FLATHEAD CATFISH
*Pylodictis olivaris*
Av., 2-4 lbs.
Common, 10-30 lbs.
Reaches, 100 lbs.

### BLUE CATFISH
*Ictalurus furcatus*
Av., 2-5 lbs.
Common, 15-25 lbs.
Reaches, 150 lbs.

### WHITE CATFISH
*Ictalurus catus*
Av., 1-2 lbs.
Common, 3 lbs.
Reaches, 12 lbs.

### BROWN BULLHEAD
*Ictalurus nebulosis*
Av., ¼-1 lb.
Common, 1-2 lbs.
Reaches, 5 lbs.

### COMMON CARP
*Cyprinus carpio*
Av., 2-5 lbs.
Common, 10-15 lbs.
Reaches, 80 lbs.

### COMMON SUCKER
*Catostomus commorsoni*
Av., ½-1½ lbs.
Common, 2-3 lbs.
Reaches, 6 lbs.

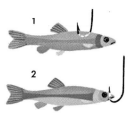

Minnows are easily netted in shallow waters with a small seine

# NATURAL BAITS

More fish are caught on natural baits than on artificials. This is true partly because more fishermen use natural baits but also because natural baits have a familiar shape, movement, or odor. Catching fish with natural baits, though requiring less skill, is still great sport.

## FRESH WATER

**MINNOWS** are the principal natural food of many fishes. Most of the many kinds of minnows used for bait measure six inches or less in length. They are caught in seines, in traps baited with bread or cornmeal, or occasionally on small hooks baited with bread, dough, or "moss." Those from still or slow-moving waters will live longer.

Minnows kept too long in a bucket will die from lack of oxygen. If the minnows begin to turn on their sides, stir or slosh

the water. Or air can be blown into the bucket through a hose, either by mouth or with a wind-driven or battery-powered air pump. Porous "breather" bait buckets help to keep water cool so that minnows are less active and hence use oxygen less rapidly. Ice placed on the bucket's lid so that water drips in as the ice melts helps to keep water cool. Many bait buckets have a detachable inner section that can be floated in the water at the fishing spot.

**HOOKING LIVE MINNOWS** For live minnow fishing, hook through muscles of back near dorsal fin (1), through both lips (2), or through tail (3). Do not hook through the backbone.

**SHINERS,** a widely distributed group of minnows, are found in ponds, lakes, and sluggish streams. The Golden Shiner, bright yellow in the breeding season, is easily reared in ponds. Common Shiners prefer streams. Many other kinds used for bait.

**DACE** are stream minnows and do not keep well in a bait bucket. Active minnows, they are used especially in fishing for trout. The Redbelly Dace, a hardy member of the group, is propagated in cool-water ponds. The Blacknose Dace is also a popular bait for trout.

**MUDMINNOWS,** closely related to pikes and pickerels, are bottom-dwellers in slow streams and in ponds. They wiggle into the mud tailfirst to hide. Mudminnows are easy to keep alive, as their oxygen needs are low. They are also lively on the hook.

**CHUBS** are large minnows and some of them are sporty panfish. River Chubs prefer large streams; Creek Chubs, the smaller, swifter streams. These and other chubs are hardy baits, and the large ones are used for Northern Pike and Muskellunge.

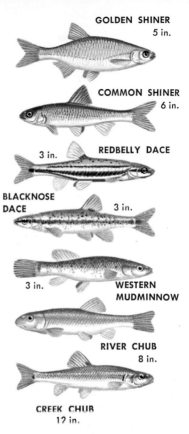

GOLDEN SHINER
5 in.

COMMON SHINER
6 in.

REDBELLY DACE
3 in.

BLACKNOSE DACE
3 in.

WESTERN MUDMINNOW
3 in.

RIVER CHUB
8 in.

CREEK CHUB
12 in.

### HOOKING DEAD MINOWS

For trolling, sew minnow onto hook by passing hook through the mouth, then out a gill opening and through the thick portion of tail. Snelled (eyeless) hooks best.

For casting, pierce body in tail region, then wrap line around body and pierce again in mid-section. Pass hook through a gill opening and out through mouth.

59

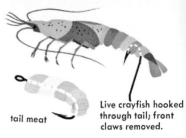

Dead crayfish, with claws intact.

tail meat

Live crayfish hooked through tail; front claws removed.

**CRAYFISH,** also called Crawdads, Craws, or Crawfish, found in ponds and streams. Caught in minnow seines by lifting rocks in riffles and letting current wash them into net, or taken in traps baited with meat. If kept wet and cool, will stay alive for a day. Hard shell is shed periodically; soft-shelled stage best for bait. Just before shedding, peel off to make a "softy." For panfish, use only tail, squeezing out meat or cracking shell to partially strip off. Meat from large pincers can also be used for panfish. For bass and other large fish, crayfish is used whole and alive, hooked through tail. Dead crayfish, threaded on hook, are good for catfish or may be fished like artificial lures for bass.

**WORMS** can be fished singly, several to a hook, or cut into pieces. For lifelike wiggle, insert hook under worm's yellowish collar. Run hook through worm twice to make secure; let end dangle. Three types used as baits are: small redworms (1-3 in.), found in manure or other organic debris; medium-sized garden worms (3-6 in.), abundant in moist, rich dirt; and nightcrawlers (to 12 in.), caught on surface in sodded areas. Will live indefinitely in damp soil, away from sun. Feed on cracker crumbs, mash, or similar foods. On trips do not crowd; carry in can or bait bucket, in damp soil or moss.

**LEECHES** live in litter on the bottom in still waters. Hooked like worms; very hardy. Good for bass, catfish.

Nightcrawler double-hooked through collar, tail dangling.

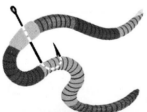

Several small worms on one hook.

Leech threaded on hook.

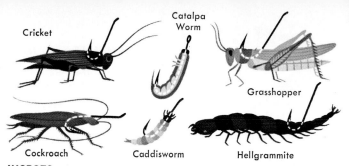

Cricket

Catalpa Worm

Grasshopper

Cockroach

Caddisworm

Hellgrammite

**INSECTS** of many kinds are fine baits. Methods of hooking interchangeable. Soft-bodied insects, such as grubs, threaded on hook like worms. Tough baits, such as hellgrammites, hooked through tail or collar.

Crickets and cockroaches can be attracted to baits, such as bread, or are easy to raise in large cans with damp sand in bottom. Feed them mash or cornmeal. Both are tender and hard to keep on hook. Grasshoppers, abundant in late summer or fall, are tougher, easier to keep alive.

Hellgrammites, the strong-jawed larvae of Dobsonflies, live under rocks in swift water. Especially good for Smallmouth Bass.

Bee or wasp larvae, catalpa worms, mealworms, or nymphs of water insects—all are good bait for bass, trout, or panfish. Caddisworms are removed from cases or cases are lightly crushed.

**FROGS AND SALAMANDERS** are good live baits for bass or other gamefish. Best bait size 2-3 in. Dead ones excellent catfish bait. To fish live, hook through lips or leg muscle, leaving them free to swim. Tadpoles, also good baits, are hooked through thick tail. Dead ones can be strung on hook. Salamanders best hooked under backbone in front of tail. Keep cool, damp.

**SALMON EGGS,** where their use is legal, are popular baits for trout or salmon. Often sold in bait shops in jars. Thread one or more on a hook.

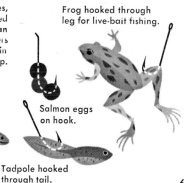

Frog hooked through leg for live-bait fishing.

Salmon eggs on hook.

Salamander hooked through tail.

Tadpole hooked through tail.

Catfish coming to stink bait.

Doughball

**DOUGHBALLS** are a favorite bait for Carp and are also good for catfish. They are made of flour, cornmeal, and water, with cotton, honey, oils, or other substances added to toughen bait and give it odor.

**STINK BAITS** are used for catfish, which find food by taste or odor. Among the many kinds are smelly cheeses, dried chicken blood, and sour clams—to which oil of anise or rhodium are added to increase odor. Bait is toughened with cotton, sponges, or similar substances. Supply can be made and then frozen.

**PORK RIND** baits are made of pig skin with the fat scraped off, then soaked in brine to preserve. They may be cut into various shapes and sizes and are either bleached or dyed. Hooked behind a spoon or fished alone, they are good baits for all freshwater gamefish and are used also in salt water.

Pork Rind Baits: strip     tadpole     frog     split tail

# SALT WATER

Among the many kinds of natural baits good in salt water, small fish are tops in popularity. But while one fisherman baits his hook with a menhaden to catch a mackerel, another baits with a mackerel to catch a shark.

**MENHADEN,** also called Mossbunkers, Hardheads, or Razor Belly Shad, are small fish of the herring family. For bait, use whole or cut. They make good chum, leaving a heavy oil slick behind boat. Menhaden spoil quickly and often must be tied to hook. Good for flatfish, kingfish, mackerels, and others.

Menhaden

head is good bait

chunk bait, with hook beneath backbone

Chum bag containing cut-up fish makes odorous slick behind boat and attracts fish. Sometimes whole fish are used for chum.

62

**MULLET** are a commercial fish of the Atlantic and Gulf. Cut large ones (12 in. or more) into fish-shaped fillets or into chunks. Fish small ones whole and alive. Mullet may be cast or trolled. With backbone removed, dead fish is limber and life-like when retrieved.

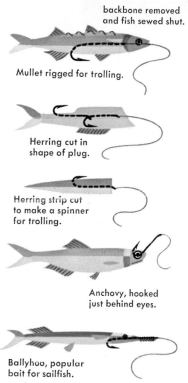

backbone removed and fish sewed shut.

Mullet rigged for trolling.

**HERRING** are small, schooling fish found in both Atlantic and Pacific. They are a major food of many fish, hence excellent bait. Can be fished whole and alive or cut into chunks or strips. Backbones sometimes cut from dead fish as with mullet (see above). Oily, herring make an excellent chum. Herring can be bought in markets, taken in nets or by hook and line.

Herring cut in shape of plug.

Herring strip cut to make a spinner for trolling.

**ANCHOVIES** are small bait fishes (4-5 in.) popular on the Pacific Coast for yellowtail, halibut, barracuda, and mackerel. Oily, they make a good chum. Usually hooked behind eyes.

Anchovy, hooked just behind eyes.

**BALLYHOO** and other half-beaks belong to the needlefish family. The traditional sailfish bait but are equally good for tunas, barracudas, and others.

Ballyhoo, popular bait for sailfish.

**EELS,** top-rated for trolling or casting for Striped Bass and other sport fish, can be fished live or dead or cut into chunks or strips. An eelskin stretched over a lead-headed metal frame is a popular casting or trolling lure called an eel bob.

**OTHER BAIT FISH** include killifish (mummichog), silversides (spearing), sand launces (sand eels), pinfish, and pigfish. They can be fished whole or as cut baits. Most fish can be used for bait. They are netted in shallows or bought in a bait store.

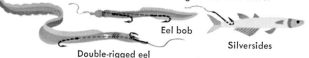

Eel bob

Double-rigged eel

Silversides

live shrimp on hook

Shrimp tail is threaded on hook.

Sandbug is hooked from underside and through shell on back.

**SHRIMP** of any species large enough to put on a hook are good as bait. Live shrimp, probably the best all-around bait for southern waters, are hooked through head or tail. Dead shrimp are cut into pieces and threaded on hook, or only tail is used. Can be bought in bait shops or in frozen packages; also netted in bays or shallows. To keep alive, place in clean, aerated water and keep them cool. Can also be used as chum.

**SANDBUGS,** or Mole Crabs, live in sand at the tide line. For small fish, use one; for large fish, several to a hook. Excellent for pompano, sheepshead, whiting.

**CRABS** of all sizes can be used in some manner as bait. Green, Blue, Lady, Hermit, Fiddler—all are good, especially for surf, drift, and still fishing. Shells of large ones are cracked and the meat stripped out. Pieces can be tied to hook with thread. Membranes where legs join body make good anchorage for hook. Crabs are best as baits just before they shed their shells; they can be "peeled." Crabs can be caught in baited traps, dug from burrows, or chased down on beach. They are sold in bait shops. To fish crabs alive, remove big claws. Crabs are easy to keep alive, even without water if kept cool.

Blue Crab

Hermit Crab in shell

Fiddler Crab

Hard-shelled crabs are hooked through the body or at edge of shell by leg membrane.

Hermit Crab is removed from shell and threaded on hook. Break off crab's large pincers.

**SHELLFISH** of all sorts—even oysters, conchs, and scallops—will catch fish. Clams are used most. Softshelled Clam (Nannygoose) is dug out with a clam hoe or rake. Observe legal limits. Shell is cracked, meat left inside. Hardshelled Clams (Quahog, Littleneck, Cherrystone) are dug from mud flats or sand beaches. Shell is pried open and meat cut out. It is hooked through snout (actually clam's foot), one or more to hook. Soft meats may be tied to hook with thread.

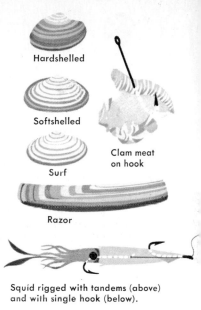

Hardshelled

Softshelled

Clam meat on hook

Surf

Razor

**SQUIDS,** or Inkfish, are common on both coasts. They can be bought in bait shops. As squid spoil quickly, they must be kept cool, frozen, or salted if not used immediately. Squids can be fished whole, used as cut bait or for chum. Tough, leathery strips stay on hook for casting or trolling with jigs or spoons. Whole ones retrieved with a twitch.

Squid rigged with tandems (above) and with single hook (below).

**WORMS** of several kinds live in shallow waters, burrowing into the sand or hiding beneath rocks. Most common for baits are Clamworms and Bloodworms. They keep well in damp seaweeds. Hook worm through head for trolling; string one or more on hook for still fishing. Good for flatfish, croakers, and others.

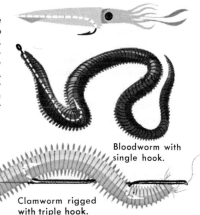

Bloodworm with single hook.

Clamworm rigged with triple hook.

# ARTIFICIAL BAITS

Some ancient fisherman discovered that fish would strike at pieces of shell or bits of bone skittered through the water. By attaching a line to this "lure" he had found a new way to catch fish. Though some artificial lures imitate a fish's natural food, many successful lures look like nothing a fish has ever seen before. Apparently their unusual action or design attracts the fish's attention.

Fishing with artificials demands more effort than does natural bait fishing. At the very least an artificial must be trolled, and many kinds give their fish-enticing action only when manipulated properly. An experienced fisherman can often catch more fish with lures than with natural baits. He fishes more water more carefully. Lures come in thousands of designs and colors. All will catch fish. Some are better than others, but none is infallible.

There are six basic types of lures: (1) *spoons*, relatively heavy and with curved or dished-out bodies, wobble but do not revolve; (2) *spinners*, relatively lightweight, with blades revolving on shafts or swivels; (3) *plugs*, with a distinct body of wood or plastic, may run deep, shallow, or on surface on retrieve; (4) *jigs*, the most versatile of all lures, have lead heads and tails of bucktail, feather, or synthetic fibers; (5) *soft plastic worms*, designed to be fished very slowly, have a lifelike feel; (6) *flies*, imitations of insects or minnows, made of feather or hair. Many lures are combinations of these basic types.

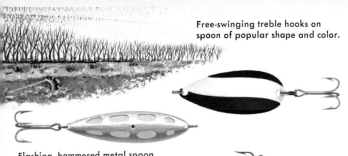

Free-swinging treble hooks on spoon of popular shape and color.

Flashing, hammered metal spoon with color windows and free-swinging treble hooks.

A gold, fly-rod size spoon, with tail flipper.

**SPOONS,** also called Wobblers, are used for trolling and casting in fresh and salt water. Their oval to round bodies may be of metal, plastic, or mother-of-pearl. The amount of wiggling and dipping a spoon does when retrieved is determined by its thickness and by its scooped-out area. Spoons range from fly rod size (1 inch) to trolling sizes of 4 to 5 inches for fresh water and up to 12 inches for salt water. Those with free-swinging treble hooks are best in open water, for they snag easily. Those with a single hook fastened rigidly ride point up and should slide over obstructions. Weedless spoons usually have a single hook equipped with a wire guard to protect hook from snagging. When fish strikes, it presses the guard out of the way. Spoons may be fished trailing a piece of pork rind, a pork chunk, feathers, or plastic strips to increase action.

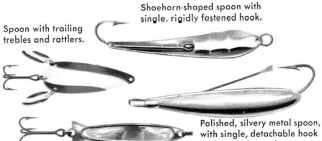

Shoehorn-shaped spoon with single, rigidly fastened hook.

Spoon with trailing trebles and rattlers.

Polished, silvery metal spoon, with single, detachable hook and a weed guard.

Mother-of-pearl spoon in shape of fish. Free-swinging trebles.

## TYPES OF SPINNER BLADES

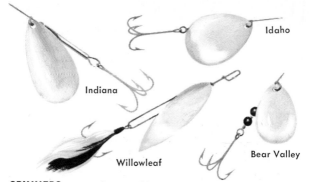

Idaho

Indiana

Willowleaf

Bear Valley

**SPINNERS** are lures with blades that whirl on shafts or swivels as they are retrieved. The hook is fastened at the end by means of a snap. Spinners can be fished alone or ahead of flies, pork rinds, or natural baits. They attract fish by commotion as well as by their flash and color. For this reason they work well in cloudy water, when silent lures are unnoticed. Spinners are made in sizes for bait casting, spinning, fly fishing, trolling.

Idaho, Indiana, and Willowleaf are the common blade shapes fished ahead of flies. June bug spinners are especially suited for slow trolling with minnows or nightcrawlers. The Bear Valley, generally fished alone, is an Idaho blade with the shaft decorated with red beads. The Colorado, an Idaho blade mounted on swivels with split rings, may be fished alone or with an artificial fly or with salmon egg bait.

Beaded Willow Leaf with fly

Colored spinner with beaded shank

June bug spinner with nightcrawler

## SURFACE PLUGS

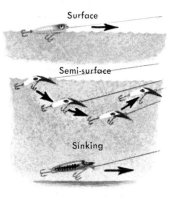

Surface

Semi-surface

Sinking

**PLUGS** are made of wood or plastic and have one or more sets of single, double, or treble hooks. Most plugs are equipped with metal lips, a gouged-out head, spinners, or other features to produce action or commotion. They are available in small sizes for fly fishing to large surf casting and trolling plugs. *Surface plugs* move along the surface in the retrieve. Some, such as dart- ers, poppers, and injured-minnow types, must be worked by jerking rod tip to give them action. Others gurgle or wobble automatically. *Semi-surface plugs* float at rest but dive when retrieved. *Sinking plugs* run deep. They sink slowly, and retrieve can be started when plug has reached desired depth. Most salt-water plugs do not have a built-in action.

## SEMI-SURFACE PLUGS

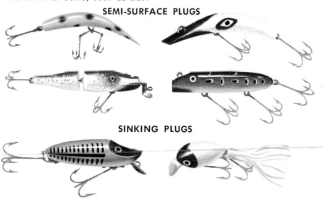

## SINKING PLUGS

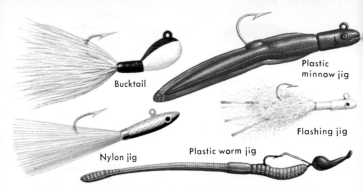

Bucktail

Plastic minnow jig

Nylon jig

Plastic worm jig

Flashing jig

**JIGS,** good in both fresh and salt water, consist of a lead head cast on a single hook. The tail is of bucktail, feathers, synthetic filaments, or soft plastic. Jigs are used in spinning, bait casting, and trolling. If head is vertical, jig runs deep; if horizontal, jig planes and can be fished in shallows without snagging. Deep-running jigs may be bounced along bottom by jerking rod tip. Heavy models are good for surf casting. "Japanese" feathers are similar to jigs but lack hooks. A wire leader is passed through a hole in lure's head, then a hook is attached.

**METAL SQUIDS** ("tin clads" or metal jigs) are made of block tin, lead, or stainless steel, and weigh ½ to 4 ounces. Used mostly in salt water. May have fixed hooks cast into body or free-swinging single, double, or treble hooks. Some are feathered. Plain hook models may be fished with pork rinds. Squidding, or surf casting with artificials, refers to use of these lures. If flattened horizontally, line planes and can be fished over rocks. Others are used for trolling or for fast retrieves. "Drails" are heavy models (to 8 ounces) used on hand lines in deep offshore water.

Minnow shape (shallow running)

Diamond-shaped squid (deep running)

Trolling squid with feather (deep running)

Block tin squid

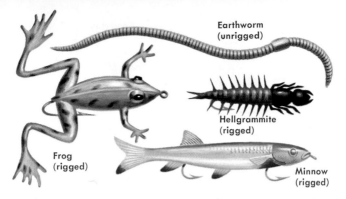

Earthworm
(unrigged)

Hellgrammite
(rigged)

Frog
(rigged)

Minnow
(rigged)

**IMITATIONS** of natural fish foods are made of molded plastics. Some plastic baits are made incredibly lifelike in feel and smell as well as in appearance. Many are sold without hooks; others are molded over a hook or a series of hooks. All imitations of natural foods must be fished like artificial lures. Some are effective if drifted.

Plastic earthworms, the most popular of the natural bait imitations, are sometimes fished behind a spinner but are also rigged with a single hook and crawled along the bottom with a slow retrieve. They are good in either fresh or salt water, as are plastic eels. Plastic eels, sold in lengths up to 20 inches, come either rigged or unrigged and are excellent lures for Striped Bass. Mackerel and squid imitations, as well as those of flyingfish, mullet, and ballyhoo, have become popular lures for trolling in salt water for marlin and other blue-water fish.

Insect imitations are good flyrod lures for fresh-water game fish and panfish. Though usually molded over hooks, some are sold without hooks. There are also imitations of frogs, minnows, crayfish, and others.

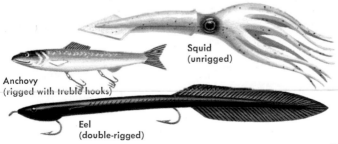

Squid
(unrigged)

Anchovy
(rigged with treble hooks)

Eel
(double-rigged)

McGinty
wing
head
tail
body
hackle

Coachman

Pink Shrimp
(salt water)

Nymph

Red-and-white
Multi-wing
(salt water)

**FLIES** may imitate insects, minnows, or crustaceans, which are the natural foods of fishes, or may be unusual, gaudy creations that attract fish either by color or by distinctive appearance. Flies are best known as lures for trout, salmon, and bass but are also used for a variety of panfish and to a limited degree in salt water. They consist of yarn, feathers, hair, tinsel, or other materials tied to a hook with thread. Some of the many thousands of patterns are centuries old. Many ardent fly fishermen carry fly-tying materials with them and tie patterns to imitate what the fish are feeding on at the moment. This is called "matching the hatch." Artificial flies are divided into two main categories: wet flies, which sink beneath the surface; and dry flies, which float. Streamer flies, surface bugs, and spinner flies are special types of flies set apart by use or by construction.

**WET FLIES** (above), generally tied on heavy hook, are sparsely dressed, with flat wings or no wings and with a soft, absorbent hackle. They imitate drowned insects, immature stages of aquatic insects, or small crustaceans. Wingless ones resembling immature insects are called *nymphs*.

**STREAMER FLIES** (below) are wet flies imitating minnows, not insects. Usually tied on a long shank hook, they are dressed with wings of saddle hackles or of bucktail. Long, slender, and lifelike when darted through water; weighted streamers may be used with spinning gear.

Black Ghost
(hackle)

Mickey Finn
(bucktail)

Royal Coachman

Bee

Furnace Spider

**DRY FLIES** (above and right) float on the surface. They are tied with stiff hackles that project at right angles to the hook's shank. The hook is usually of light wire. Dry flies imitate either living or dead insects. They are fished in the natural drift of the water and are not given action by the angler.

Brown Bivisible

**SURFACE BUGS** (right) have lightweight bodies of cork, plastic, or hair. They may imitate living things, such as moths, frogs, or crippled minnows, or may be simply attractors. One type with a concave face produces a popping sound when twitched on the surface. Popular for bass.

Popper
(cork-bodied)

Hair Mouse

**SPINNER FLIES** (below) are large wet flies dressed with a hackle or with bucktail and tied on a ringed-eye hook. Spinner flies are usually wingless and are designed to be fished behind a spinner. They are exceptionally good lures for fresh-water bass but are also a highly effective combination for panfish.

Moth

Feather Minnow

Yellow Miller
(with spinner)

# TACKLE AND ITS USE

Tackle consists of rod, reel, line, leader, sinker, hook—all the manufactured items a fisherman uses in catching fish. Artificial baits or lures (p. 66) are also tackle but are described separately in this book because of their similarity to natural baits (p. 58) in action, appearance, and use. Accessories (p. 106) are equipment that help directly or indirectly but are not essential for catching fish.

While some kinds of tackle are designed for a specific type of fishing, they may serve a variety of purposes or be used interchangeably. Tackle that is made especially to cast artificial baits can be used also for still fishing, for trolling, or even for surf fishing. Light fresh-water equipment will catch fish in salt water but may not always do as well on larger salt-water fish as heavier gear, which is made also of materials resistant to salt-water corrosion. Simple makeshift tackle, such as the fabled willow pole, string, and bent pin, will catch fish, but properly selected tackle in skilled hands will take more fish and give greater satisfaction to the fisherman. In these pages, the basic tackle, consisting of rod, reel, and line, is described first generally and comparatively, then in greater detail in the units for which it is designed to be used.

| TYPES OF TACKLE | PRINCIPAL AND OTHER USES |
|---|---|
| Fly | casting flies, still fishing, fresh and salt |
| Spinning | casting lures, trolling, still fishing, fresh and salt |
| Bait and Spin Casting | casting lures, trolling, still fishing, fresh and salt |
| Surf | surf casting, squidding, salt water |
| Bay and Big Game | bottom fishing and trolling, salt water |

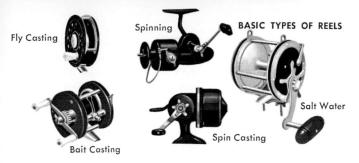

Fly Casting

Spinning

**BASIC TYPES OF REELS**

Salt Water

Bait Casting

Spin Casting

**REELS** are devices on which line is stored. The line can be released or retrieved as needed. A reel may be a simple ungeared spool equipped with a handle for cranking and set in a frame. The single-action fly reel is of this type. Or a reel may be a precision mechanism with multiple gears and even an electric-motor-driven spool, as in some big-game reels. The principal types of reels are fly, bait casting, spin casting, spinning, and salt water, all manufactured in a wide range of sizes. Most reels are made of aluminum alloys or of chrome-plated brass, with some gears and many other parts made of plastic.

**STAR DRAG,** named for the star-shaped adjusting wheel at the base of the reel handle, consists of a series of metal and leather or composition discs that slip less freely as the star wheel is tightened. This is the most common of drag adjustments that control the tension on a reel spool.

**LEVEL WIND** devices, found on nearly all bait-casting reels, consist of a worm gear, or carriage screw, and a pawl that moves a line guide back and forth across front of spool so that line is wound on evenly. Movement of level wind mechanism is synchronized with spool's gears.

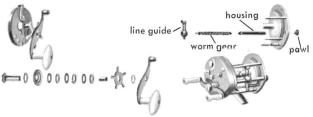

line guide

housing

worm gear

pawl

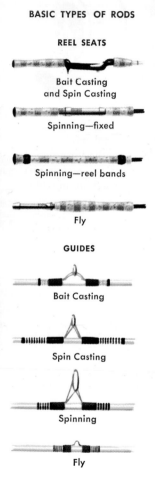

**BASIC TYPES OF RODS**

**REEL SEATS**

Bait Casting
and Spin Casting

Spinning—fixed

Spinning—reel bands

Fly

**GUIDES**

Bait Casting

Spin Casting

Spinning

Fly

**RODS** furnish the leverage for casting and for setting the hook. The rod's flexibility, called its "action," puts the sport in playing a fish. A rod's action, ranging from limber to stiff, is determined by the taper, thickness and material of which the rod is made. Wood, steel, split-bamboo—a variety of materials—have been used, but most rods are now made of hollow fiberglass or of spun glass impregnated with plastic. Strong for their weight and uniform in action throughout their length, glass rods give long service and require little care. Rods may be made in one piece or, for portability, in two or more sections joined by ferrules. Identifying features of some principal rods are shown.

**LINES** range from sewing thread for catching bait minnows to ⅜-inch ropes for hauling in sharks or jewfish. Most lines are rated in pounds test: that is, the maximum weight in pounds they will lift without breaking. They may also be designated by their diameter in cross section. Some monofilaments are colored for visibility to the fisherman, but they become nearly invisible to the fish underwater.

# FISHING LINES

| MATERIAL | ADVANTAGES | DISADVANTAGES |
|---|---|---|
| Braided Nylon | Smooth finish, small diameter, high knot strength, resistance to rot, needs little care. Good for bait casting, squidding. | Low specific gravity, excessive stretch, some tendency to fray, comparatively high drag in water. |
| Braided Silk | Very smooth finish, high knot strength, excellent spooling, low stretch. Good line for bait casting. | Comparatively large diameter for test, very subject to rot, requires great deal of care for long life. |
| Braided Dacron | Very small diameter, low drag in water, high specific gravity. Good line for trolling, bottom fishing, or bait casting. | Often too water-repellent and excessively dry, making it hot on thumb in casting; knot strength lower than silk or nylon. |
| Round Monofilament | Low drag in wind and water, low visibility to fish, good knot strength. Good for spinning, trolling and bait casting. | Tends to be stiff in all but lightest tests, very "dry" to cast with revolving spool reels. Wears guides rapidly. |
| Wire Lines and Lead-cored Braids | Fast sinking without sinkers. Especially good for deep trolling. | Hard to pay off reel without backlashing. Tend to kink. |

**HAND LINES,** used without either rod or reel, can be efficient fish catchers. With practice, a fisherman can cast long distances by twirling the sinker to build momentum, then letting it go at the right moment. Coiling the line neatly is the secret of casting success. Hand lines are used mostly in still fishing or fishing on the bottom by drifting. They are good also for fishing from bridges, piers and party boats. While used most commonly for bait fishing, hand lines are fine also for trolling with artificial lures. They are the common tackle of commercial fishermen in both fresh and salt water for getting fish out of the water fast, with little concern about "sport."

**CANE POLES** are simple fishing rods, ranging from 7 to 15 feet long and varying in action from whippy to fairly stiff. The line may be tied only to the tip of the pole or, in some cases, secured also to the butt end to prevent the loss of a fish and tackle if the pole breaks. The line may be monofilament, braided or solid wire, or braided silk, linen, nylon, or dacron. Monofilament is probably best for general use. As a rule, the line should not be much longer than the pole, as longer lines are difficult to manage. Some poles are rigged with guides and with simple line-holding reels.

Cane poles are commonly used in bait fishing for fresh-water panfish. They are good also for "jigging" small bucktails for crappies and perch or in fishing with flies, spoons, pork rinds, or other artificials for bass or pickerel, especially in weedy waters. In salt water, cane poles are used from piers and bridges to catch sea trout, mackerel, and salt-water panfish. Stout poles rigged with wire line are effective in dragging large snook and other sizable fish from the deep holes around barnacle-encrusted pilings or similar lairs.

**HAND LINES** are usually made of twisted or braided linen or of nylon. They are coarse textured, making them easy to hold. Though harder to handle, heavy monofilament hand lines give long service. For salt-water fishing, linen lines are often treated with coal tar or creosote as a preservative. For big groupers, sharks, or other large fish, fishermen use giant-sized hooks with a chain leader and a rope line.

ferrule

Two-piece Metal Pole, with guides

**HAND LINES**

salt water

fresh water

big hook with chain leader on a rope line

**A CANE POLE** is simply a stalk of bamboo of suitable size and length. Long poles may be cut in half and ferruled in the middle to make them easier to carry. Modern "cane poles" are made of glass or of metal. Some come in sections joined by ferrules; others telescope. Simple poles are a first step in getting more sport from a fish. Even a small panfish's antics are amplified at the end of a pole as opposed to hauling in the same size fish on a hand line.

Telescoping Glass Pole

Cane Pole, line tied at tip

Simple Line-holding Reel

**SPINNING,** which originated in Europe, is by far the most popular fishing method in America. In spinning, the line simply slips, or "spins," from the end of the reel spool, which does not revolve as it does in a bait-casting reel. Spinning is a highly versatile method and can be used for casting artificial lures, for trolling or for natural-bait fishing. A wide range of lure and bait weights can be used with spinning tackle. With a spinning outfit, smooth casting can be mastered quickly, and the playing of fish is easy.

**SPINNING REELS** are manufactured in a wide range of sizes and styles, but all have a number of features in common. All true spinning reels have an open-faced spool. They are mounted below the rod handle, with the axis of the spool more or less parallel with the rod. For right-handed casters, the crank is on the left side. Left-handed models are also available. All should hold at least 100 yards of line, which is wound on the spool by a revolving bail, finger or stud. The spool is moved in and out by a center shaft to cross-wind the line as it is retrieved. Quality spinning reels have a line guide or roller of stainless steel or hard alloy to minimize line wear. Adjustable drags, usually regulated by wing nuts at the front of the spool, can be set so that large fish can be handled safely with very light lines.

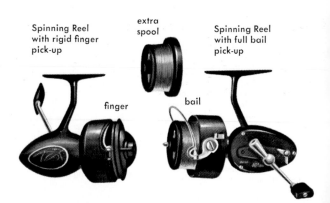

Spinning Reel with rigid finger pick-up

extra spool

Spinning Reel with full bail pick-up

finger

bail

**SPINNING RODS** range in length from 5 to 10 feet, with 6- to 7-foot lengths most popular. The butt guide is very large to gather the first large loops of line that spin from the reel during the cast. On salt-water spinning rods, the butt guide may be as much as 3 inches in diameter. The guides diminish in size to the tip, but to minimize line friction in casting, all guides are large compared to those on bait casting or fly rods. A fast-taper spinning rod—with a powerful butt tapering to a limber tip—provides the best all-round action. Most spinning rods are made of glass, either hollow or solid. A few expensive rods are made of split-bamboo. Nearly all spinning rods today have fixed reel seats—that is, a knurled ring that can be screwed tightly on a threaded section to hold the reel firmly in place. The grips are usually of cork.

**SPINNING LINES** are made exclusively of solid synthetic monofilaments that are round in cross section. Monofilaments cast better and wear longer than braids, and they are also less visible to the fish. Stren, nylon, and imported synthetics are the most popular. Most spinning lines are produced in neutral translucent shades. However, some that are brightly colored or even fluorescent in the air become nearly invisible to the fish underwater. Spinning lines range from ½- to 20-pound test. Heavier sizes are too stiff to cast well, even with large lures.

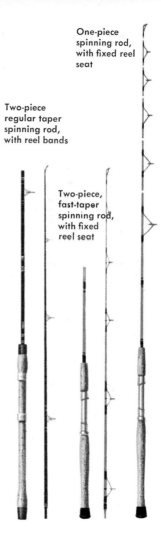

One-piece spinning rod, with fixed reel seat

Two-piece regular taper spinning rod, with reel bands

Two-piece, fast-taper spinning rod, with fixed reel seat

# HOW TO CAST WITH SPINNING TACKLE

Hold the spinning rod slightly above a horizontal position, with the lure hanging down a few inches from the tip. Catch the line on the ball of your forefinger and let the weight of the lure hold it there as you open the bail (or finger) to release the line. Now bring the rod up sharply to slightly past the vertical position and immediately snap it forward again. As the rod comes down near the horizontal, straighten your forefinger to release the line, and the cast is underway. When the lure reaches the target, drop your finger to the edge of the spool to stop the line from spooling off the reel.

When fishing with spinning tackle, always set the reel drag so that it slips under a tension considerably below the breaking strength of the line. If the drag is set too tight, the line will break when a fish makes a sudden lunge. Never try to wind a fish in while it is taking line. This will result in a twisted line and commonly loses the fish. When either casting or still fishing, do not engage the anti-reverse lock until a fish is hooked. In trolling, keep the anti-reverse lock engaged.

**SIDE CAST** is used where an overhead cast is not possible. With wrist, move the rod from side to side and release lure in low flight in direction of target.

**FLIP CAST** is useful in fishing tight spots. With 3 or 4 feet of line out, grasp the hook by its bend. Pull rod down and then release hook to let it shoot out.

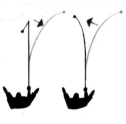

1. Hold rod with second and third fingers straddling reel leg, the forefinger holding line.

2. Start with rod near 10 o'clock position, the lure hanging a few inches from tip. Open bail.

3. Bring rod up sharply to between 12 and 1 o'clock position, Forefinger still holds line.

4. Momentum bends rod back to develop power to propel lure forward on the cast.

5. Snap rod forward, gaining more power. Do not apply power past 11 o'clock position.

6. Release line by straightening finger. Lure momentum pulls line from reel spool.

**FLY FISHING,** one of the oldest forms of sport fishing with artificial lures, probably furnishes more fishing pleasure per pound of fish landed than any other method. The usual lures are the virtually weightless flies (pp. 72-73), though very small plugs, spoons, and other lures can also be used. Fly casting is easier than bait casting, though not quite so easy as spinning. In some situations, as when fish are feeding on a hatch of insects, tiny fly-rod lures may be the only artificial baits that will catch fish.

**FLY LINES** provide the weight needed to cast extremely light lures. Stiff, powerful rods require heavier lines than do light, limber rods. Fly lines are made of braided silk, nylon, or dacron impregnated and coated with oil or plastic to give them a smooth finish. Some have hollow cores or air bubbles in the finish to make them float in fishing surface flies or lures; others are weighted to make them sink quickly in fishing deep. Level lines are the same diameter from end to end. Double tapers have small diameter ends for delicacy and heavy midsections for weight. When one end becomes worn, the line is reversed. In torpedo tapers (weight forward), the heavy front section makes casting easy. As fly lines are bulky, they should be used with long leaders to deceive the fish (pp. 98-99).

| SYMBOLS FOR STANDARD FLY LINE | | |
|---|---|---|
| DT = Double Taper | | |
| WF = Weight Forward (Torpedo Taper) | | |
| F = Floating Line | | |
| S = Sinking Line | | |
| I = Intermediate Line (floats or sinks) | | |

| STANDARD FLY LINE WEIGHTS | | | | | |
|---|---|---|---|---|---|
| # | Wt.* | Range** | # | Wt. | Range |
| 1 | 60 | 54-66 | 7 | 185 | 177-193 |
| 2 | 80 | 74-86 | 8 | 210 | 202-218 |
| 3 | 100 | 94-106 | 9 | 240 | 230-250 |
| 4 | 120 | 114-126 | 10 | 280 | 270-290 |
| 5 | 140 | 134-136 | 11 | 330 | 318-342 |
| 6 | 160 | 152-168 | 12 | 380 | 368-392 |

*Weight is in grains based on first 30 ft. of line exclusive of taper tip.
**Range allows for acceptable manufacturing tolerances.

DT    9    S    DACRON
TIP    30 ft. 240 GRAINS

DT    9    F    NYLON
TIP    30 ft. 240 GRAINS

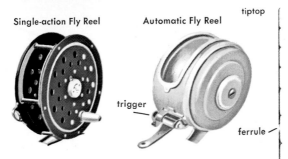

Single-action Fly Reel     Automatic Fly Reel

trigger

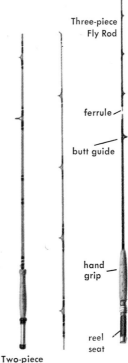

tiptop

ferrule

Three-piece
Fly Rod

ferrule

butt guide

hand
grip

reel
seat

Two-piece
Fast Taper Fly Rod

**FLY REELS** generally have narrow spools of large diameter. Because of the narrow-width spool, a level-wind mechanism is not necessary, and the large spool diameter makes possible a faster retrieve. In single-action reels, the spool rotates once for each turn of the handle. Double multipliers speed retrieves. Automatic reels hold less line and have spring to retrieve line at the touch of a lever or trigger.

**FLY RODS** are designed to handle the heavy fly lines that provide the weight for casting flies or other lightweight lures. The reel seat is located behind the grip to make it easier to strip line from the reel. Fly rods vary in length from 6½ to 17 feet; in weight, from 1 to 20 ounces. Popular sizes weigh 4 to 7 ounces, in 7½- to 9-foot lengths. Light but very powerful, fast-taper models handle a wider range of line sizes. Most fly rods today are made of hollow fiberglass, but split-bamboo is still fairly popular. Most fly rods come in 2 or 3 pieces, the sections being connected by ferrules.

A fly rod may be gripped with the thumb at the side, or with the thumb on top of the handle. Many anglers alternate to rest their wrists.

**HOW TO FLY CAST**  Let out about 25 feet of line in front of you and then, holding the rod as shown above, strip off a few more feet and hold it with your left hand. Raise the rod slowly until the line in front of you is free of slack. At this point the rod should be a little above the horizontal. Now bring the rod up briskly to the vertical position, and pause as the line soars into the air behind you. It may help to look back over your shoulder to watch the line on the back cast. Start your forward cast when the line has nearly straightened but has not begun to fall. Bring the rod forward with the same force used on the back cast, easing off on the power well before the rod reaches the horizontal. As the rod snaps straight, the line will be propelled out in front of you. While the line is still moving fast, release the slack line held in the left hand for greater distance.

In fly fishing for trout and panfish, use a light-action rod with a small single-action or an automatic reel. For bass, select a rod that will handle heavier lines and bulkier lures and either a single-action or automatic reel. For salmon or salt-water species, use a powerful rod, at least 9 feet long, and a large reel filled with backing line for the long runs made by these fish.

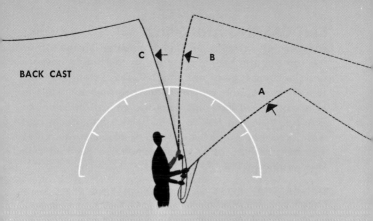

**BACK CAST**

Start the back cast (above) with the rod between 1 and 2 o'clock, slowly lifting the rod to eliminate slack line (A). Raise the rod briskly to near 12 o'clock (B). Stop the rod at about 12 o'clock and pause while line straightens out in air behind you (C).

When the back cast has nearly straightened out (below), bring the rod forward with force (D). Ease off on the power between 1 and 2 o'clock and let line roll forward (E). As line reaches maximum speed, release slack in left hand for more distance (F).

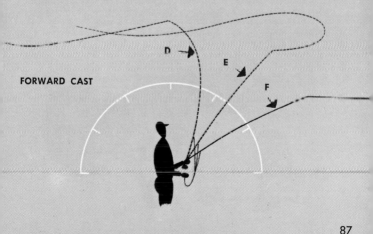

**FORWARD CAST**

**BAIT CASTING AND SPIN CASTING** are technically similar. In both, the reel is mounted on the top of the rod handle, the thumb controls the line in casting, and the same type of rod may be used. But in bait casting, the reel spool revolves as the line runs out, while in spin casting the line slips from the end of the spool as in a true spinning reel (p. 80). Bait casting works best with lures that weigh more than $\frac{3}{8}$ of an ounce. Lures weighing as little as $\frac{1}{8}$ of an ounce can be used with spin-casting tackle.

**BAIT-CASTING REELS** have a rather wide spool that revolves four times for each turn of the handle. In most kinds, the reel handles turn on the cast, but in some, the handles can be disengaged for free-spooling. Nearly all bait-casting reels have a level-wind mechanism to spool the line evenly and a "click" that can be set when not casting to keep the spool from turning freely. On some reels, a star drag allows the line to be pulled from the reel under tension when playing large fish.

**SPIN-CASTING REELS** are a modified type of spinning reel, with the spool enclosed in a conical cover. The line passes through a hole in the center of the cover. A thumb-operated trigger, or push button, at the rear releases the line for the cast and, when pushed again, stops the flow of line from the spool. Like bait-casting reels, most spin-casting reels are reeled in with the right hand. All have drag mechanisms for smooth playing of fish. Gear ratios vary from 2 to 1 to 4 to 1.

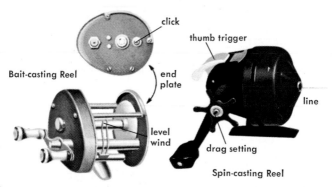

click

Bait-casting Reel

end plate

level wind

thumb trigger

line

drag setting

Spin-casting Reel

**CASTING RODS** range from 4 to 7 feet. Average length of a true bait-casting rod, which has low guides, is 5 feet; of a spin-casting rod, which has large, high-bridged guides, 6½ feet. A fast-taper spin-casting rod can be used also with bait-casting reel, handling lures from ⅛ to 1 ounce. Bait-casting rod can be used for spin casting but does not cast lightweight lures. Both rods usually have detachable handles with offset, locking reel seats. Most are of hollow glass; solid glass, split-bamboo, and metal alloys are used also.

**CASTING LINES** are made of synthetic monofilament or of braided synthetics, such as nylon or dacron. Braids testing from 10 to 30 pounds are best for bait casting, but monofilaments up to 15-pound test may be used. For spin casting, use spinning lines of 6- or 10-pound test. The color for a braided casting line is a matter of personal choice, but black is the most popular.

### LINE TYPES AND COLORS

Braided
| black |

| tan |

| camouflaged |

Monofilaments
mist — oval

fluorescent — round

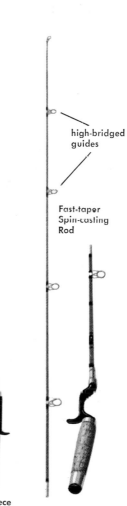

high-bridged guides

Fast-taper Spin-casting Rod

Two-piece Bait-casting Rod

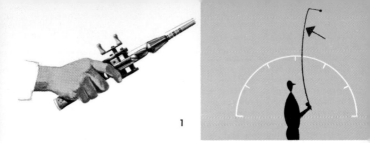

**BAIT CASTING** 1. Hold the rod at about the 2 o'clock position, with reel handle facing up.

2. With a smooth wrist action, lift the rod sharply to about the 12 o'clock position.

# HOW TO BAIT CAST

Hold the rod slightly above the horizontal, with the reel handles facing upward and with the lure hanging a few inches from the tip. Bring the rod up sharply to a vertical position but keep wrist straight. The weight of the lure will bend the rod tip. Snap the rod forward again with a smooth flex of your wrist. As the rod straightens, ease your thumb pressure to allow the spool to turn. Keep the reel handles up. Apply a light thumb pressure on spool to prevent it from turning faster than line goes out, causing a backlash or line tangle on the spool. When lure reaches target, thumb the spool to stop cast and to cause lure to drop.

3. As the lure bends rod tip back, give forward cast power with wrist to 1 o'clock.

4. Lift thumb slightly so spool can turn and let line out. Thumb spool to stop cast at the target.

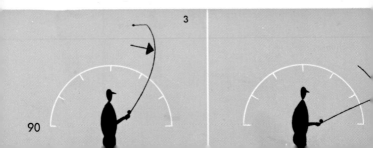

**SPIN CASTING** 1. Hold rod at about 2 o'clock; push trigger with thumb to release line.

2. Snap rod upward briskly to about 12 o'clock, keeping the trigger pressed with thumb.

## HOW TO SPIN CAST

Spin casting is easier than bait casting because it is not necessary to use thumb control to prevent backlashes. But without the delicate control possible with the thumb, there is less accuracy. To spin cast, point the rod at a spot over the target, letting the lure hang a few inches below the tip. Release the line for casting by pressing the thumb trigger, turning the crank backward if necessary. Keep your thumb on the trigger as you lift rod sharply to vertical. Flick it forward again immediately, using your wrist. As rod straightens, release thumb trigger to let line go out. To stop cast, press trigger. Then turn crank to put reel in gear for retrieve.

3. Bring rod down and forward with wrist action, applying power to about 1 o'clock.

4. Release trigger to let line go out for cast. Press trigger again to stop lure at target.

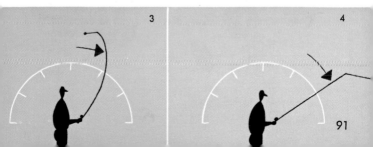

Surf-casting Rod

reel seat

ferrule

butt    hand grip                    hand grip

**SURF CASTING** can be done with any type of tackle,
but heavy surf gear is best where waves roll in high. It
takes long casts to reach the first line of breakers where
game fish often feed. The long surf rod helps hold line
high to clear foaming breakers, and the sturdy reel with-
stands strains of casting heavy weights and fighting
fish. Many types of artificial lures can be used for squidding, a form of surf fishing, but most surf fisherman
prefer to fish on bottom with natural baits.

**SURF-CASTING REELS** have
wide spools that hold at least
200 yards of line. They have a
retrieve ratio of at least 3 to 1
and are free-spooling for easy
casting. All have star drags to
allow fish to pull line out under
desired tension. Many models
have level-wind devices.

**SURF SPINNING REELS** are
built like conventional spinning
reels (p. 80), but are larger and
heavier. Gears and drags are
heavy duty. Their spools may
hold 200 to 500 yards of 8- to
15-pound test monofilament.
Most have bail-type pick-ups
and hardened line rollers.

free-spool lever

star drag

Surf-casting Reel

Surf-spinning Reel

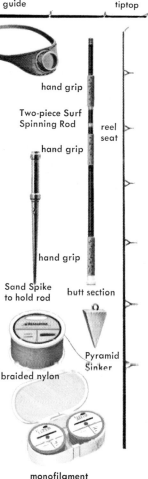

guide                                    tiptop

Rod Belt for
surf fishing

**SURF-CASTING RODS** have
a long tip and a long handle.
The tip, made of glass or of split-
bamboo, is usually from 6 to 7
feet long and weighs 7 to 14
ounces. The tip attaches to a
28- to 32-inch hardwood handle,
which has two grips—one just behind the screw-locking reel seat
and another at the butt end. This
arrangement gives leverage for
the two-handed long casts. Most
surf-spinning rods, which are 8
to 10 feet long and weigh 8 to
12 ounces, are made of glass
and consist of two pieces. They
are joined or ferruled near the
middle or a few inches above
the handle. The handle has cork
grips above and below the reel
seat. Guides on surf-spinning
rods are very large to minimize
line friction in casting.

hand grip

Two-piece Surf
Spinning Rod

reel
seat

hand grip

hand grip

Sand Spike
to hold rod

butt section

**LINES** for surf fishing are
usually of braided nylon or dacron, but monofilaments can be
used by skilled casters. For surf
casting, braided nylon from 18-
to 45-pound test is popular. On
the other hand, because of small
diameter and high specific grav-
ity, braided dacron's low water
resistance makes it excellent for
bottom fishing in heavy, foaming
surf. For spinning, use only
monofilaments from 6- to 20-
pound test.

Pyramid
Sinker

braided nylon

monofilament

93

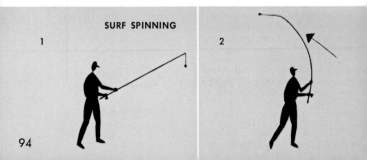

**HOW TO SURF CAST**   Before attempting a cast with a revolving-spool surf reel, wet your line. This prevents it from burning your thumb on the cast. Shift reel into free spool and put thumb firmly on the spool. Let out 2 or 3 feet of line, and hold the rod pointed low opposite the direction of your cast, the sinker resting on the ground. Now bring the rod up with a powerful overhead sweep, pulling downward with your left hand and pushing upward with your right. As the rod comes up past the vertical, ease your thumb pressure and let the spool turn. Let the line run out under your thumb; removing your thumb will cause a backlash. As the sinker hits the water, thumb spool hard. Surf spinning is done with same motions, using forefinger instead of thumb to control line.

**SURF SPINNING**

1

2

**SURF CASTING** 1. Grasp rod firmly and stand with feet wide apart for good balance. Surf casting requires power as well as proper timing.

2. Face at right angle to direction of cast; bring rod up with overhand sweep; push up with right hand, pull down with left.

3. Follow through; apply power past the vertical and turn your body in direction of cast to develop more speed and power.

4. Lift thumb slightly, easing pressure on the spool and allowing it to turn. Control speed with gentle thumbing. Stop spool the instant sinker hits water.

**SURF SPINNING** may be done like surf casting (p. 94) or with a backcast, shown below. 1. Holding rod as shown, catch line with forefinger and open the bail.

2. Grip rod firmly with right hand, fingers straddling reel leg, left hand on lower grip. Snap rod back to position past vertical.

3. Sweep rod forward, pushing with right hand and pulling with left to build the power and speed to bring out spring action of rod.

4. Release line by straightening forefinger and letting line spin from spool. Drop forefinger to the edge of the spool to stop the cast where desired.

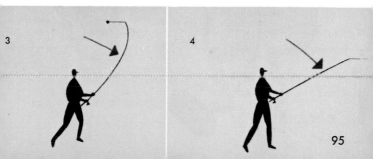

**SALT-WATER TACKLE**  Big-game fishing is done largely on charter boats with the tackle, bait and know-how provided by the charter-boat captain. It is less expensive for the occasional fisherman to pay the charter fees, ranging to well over $100 a day, than it is to invest in the equipment needed for big-game fishing. General salt-water fishing—trolling, drift fishing, bottom fishing and live-bait fishing—can be done with relatively inexpensive tackle and boat equipment.

**REELS** for big-game and general salt-water fishing are similar in many features. All have free-spool clutches turned on or off with a lever, oversize crank grips, and heavy-duty spools. Most have star drags, located beneath the handle hub and adjusted by a star-shaped wheel. Some high-priced big-game reels have drags with calibrated settings. Most general-purpose salt-water reels, or bay reels, are double-multiplying (the spool revolving twice for each crank of the handle), with relatively narrow spools and bakelite end-plates. Big-game reels have heavier frames and smoother drags, and some have gearshifts for variable retrieve ratios. Bay reels hold 100 to 400 yards of line; big-game reels, to 1,000 yards of 130-pound dacron.

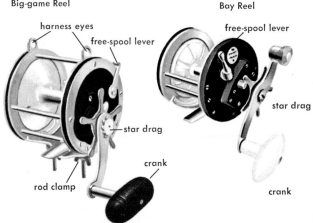

Big-game Reel

harness eyes

free-spool lever

star drag

rod clamp

crank

Bay Reel

free-spool lever

star drag

crank

**RODS** for bottom fishing, trolling and big-game fishing range in length from 5 to 9 feet. Big-game rods are built of high quality split-bamboo, laminated wood, or glass. Most have roller tops and high-bridged roller guides to reduce line friction. Tips on big-game rods are 5 feet long and weigh from 3 to 40 ounces. The butt section varies from 14 to 24 inches in length, depending on the tip weight. Reel seats are double-locking, and a notched butt cap fits into a gimbal (socket) on the boat's fighting chair. Trolling rods are similar to big-game rods but generally lack the heavy-duty features. Boat rods, used with boy reels, are usually made of glass and have wooden handles and plain guides. They vary from stiff 5-foot models to whippy 9-footers. Most are in two pieces, ferruled in the middle.

**LINES** for salt-water fishing range from 12- to 130-pound test. Monofilaments and braided dacron have become the standard lines for most big-game fishing. Dacron, monofilaments, and braided wire are used in trolling, with wire the best for fishing deep. For general salt-water use, braided nylon is best.

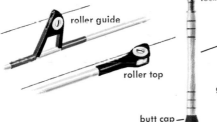

roller guide

roller top

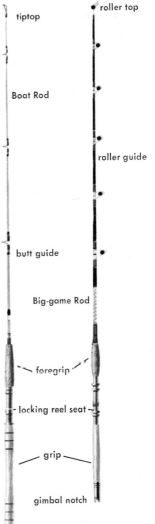

tiptop

roller top

Boat Rod

roller guide

butt guide

Big-game Rod

foregrip

locking reel seat

grip

gimbal notch

butt cap

**LEADERS** may be used to make a nearly invisible connection between the line and the lure, thus helping to deceive the fish. Other kinds of leaders provide extra strength and toughness to withstand the cutting of sharp teeth and gill covers or the sawing abrasion on rocks, logs, pilings, or other underwater objects. Finally, and often overlooked, leaders may enhance the action of lures. Some lures, in fact, do not work properly unless attached to a leader; others will foul their hooks on the line unless a short, stiff wire leader is used.

**FLY-CASTING LEADERS** are almost invisible. They also make it possible to land a fly lightly on the water. Nylon, Stren, and other synthetic monofilaments have largely replaced silkworm gut, the classic material for fly-casting leaders. The synthetics are stronger and more uniform in diameter than gut, and they do not have to be soaked to soften them before they can be used. A fly-casting leader may be of equal diameter, called level, throughout its length, but the most effective leader is tapered from a heavy butt section to a slim terminal section, called the tippet. A tapered leader can be made by tying together (with blood knots, p. 114) a series of short, gradually lighter strands, as shown below. Some commercial leaders are reduced in diameter from butt to tippet without being knotted. Fly leaders average 7 to 9 feet long, but may run to 15 or 20 feet.

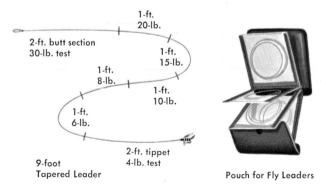

1-ft. 20-lb.

2-ft. butt section 30-lb. test

1-ft. 15-lb.

1-ft. 8-lb.

1-ft. 10-lb.

1-ft. 6-lb.

2-ft. tippet 4-lb. test

9-foot Tapered Leader

Pouch for Fly Leaders

**BAIT-CASTING and SPINNING LEADERS** serve mainly to protect the line. They take the brunt of the wear and tear. Made of plain or plastic-coated braided wire, or of solid stainless steel, they range in length from 6 to 12 inches. A safety snap at the end makes the changing of hooks or lures swift and simple, and a swivel between the line and the leader prevents twisting. When bait casting with a braided line, which is highly visible, a 4- to 6-foot monofilament leader may be used for deception. If a light-test monofilament line is used, a short mono leader of slightly stronger test than the line serves as a good shock absorber.

**BOTTOM - FISHING LEADERS,** of monofilament or of solid or braided wire, protect the line from fish's teeth and also locate hook properly. Often the snell on hook serves as leader.

**BIG-GAME FISHING LEADERS** range from 6 to 15 feet in length and 70- to 500-pound test. Most commonly used materials are tinned steel (piano wire) or solid stainless steel wire. Stainless wire resists corrosion better than tinned steel but is not as strong and also tends to kink after being stretched. Tinned wire is shiny, however, and may reflect light in clear water. Big-game fishing leaders may be made also of heavy monofilament or of cabled stainless steel. Cabled wire is best where tests over 150 pounds are needed.

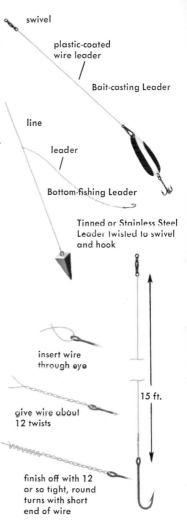

swivel

plastic-coated wire leader

Bait-casting Leader

line

leader

Bottom-fishing Leader

Tinned or Stainless Steel Leader twisted to swivel and hook

insert wire through eye

give wire about 12 twists

15 ft.

finish off with 12 or so tight, round turns with short end of wire

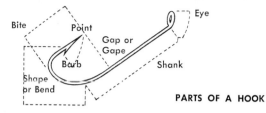

**PARTS OF A HOOK**

**HOOKS** catch the fish. All other tackle serves only to get the hook to a fish's mouth. Choice of which of the many fishhook styles to use depends on the kind of fishing and on personal preference. Buy hooks made by a reputable manufacturer. Cheap hooks have poor points and may be made of a metal that breaks, bends, or rusts quickly; they lose fish. Check the eye. It should be pulled tightly against the shank, leaving no cutting edge. Oval or forged shanks indicate an extra step in manufacturing, as do hollow or rolled points. In salt water use hooks made of nickel alloy or "tinned" steel. Salt water rusts japanned or lacquered hooks rapidly. Hone the points of hooks often; they are likely to be dulled in use. New styles are varieties of basic types (pp. 102-103).

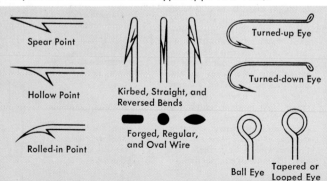

Spear Point

Hollow Point

Rolled-in Point

Kirbed, Straight, and Reversed Bends

Forged, Regular, and Oval Wire

Turned-up Eye

Turned-down Eye

Ball Eye

Tapered or Looped Eye

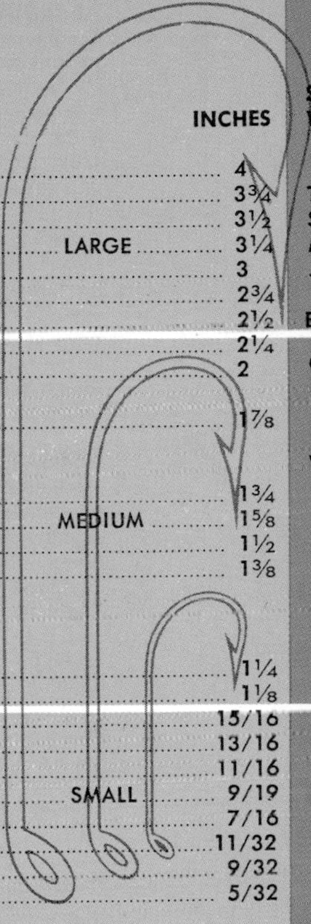

| FRESH WATER | HOOK SIZE | | INCHES | SALT WATER |
|---|---|---|---|---|
| | 13/0 | | 4 | |
| | 12/0 | | 3¾ | TUNA |
| | 11/0 | | 3½ | SAILFISH |
| | 10/0 | LARGE | 3¼ | MARLIN |
| | 9/0 | | 3 | |
| | 8/0 | | 2¾ | TARPON |
| | 7/0 | | 2½ | BARRACUDA |
| MUSKIE | 6/0 | | 2¼ | |
| PIKE | 5/0 | | 2 | CHANNEL BASS |
| BASS | | | | STRIPED BASS |
| | 4/0 | | 1⅞ | BONEFISH |
| | | | | BLUEFISH |
| | | | | WEAKFISH |
| | 3/0 | | 1¾ | |
| WALLEYE | 2/0 | MEDIUM | 1⅝ | CROAKER |
| | 1/0 | | 1½ | FLOUNDER |
| PICKEREL | 1½ | | 1⅜ | BLACKFISH |
| | | | | PORGY |
| | | | | POMPANO |
| BULLHEAD | 1 | | 1¼ | |
| | 2 | | 1⅛ | |
| PERCH | 4 | | 15/16 | KELP BASS |
| TROUT | 6 | | 13/16 | SNAPPER |
| CRAPPIE | 8 | | 11/16 | SMELT |
| BLUEGILL | 10 | SMALL | 9/19 | |
| SUNFISH | 12 | | 7/16 | |
| | 14 | | 11/32 | |
| | 16 | | 9/32 | |
| | 20 | | 5/32 | |

**HOOK SIZES** range from 22/0 or larger (for sharks) to novelty size 32. Above chart shows size of hooks in round bend style with standard length shanks. Most manufacturers use this system. Avoid using hooks that are too large. A big fish can be caught on a small hook more easily than a small fish on a large hook.

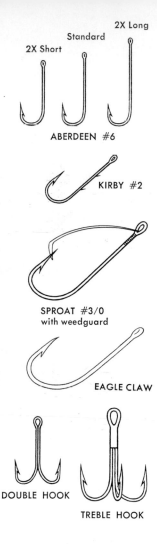

2X Short | Standard | 2X Long

ABERDEEN #6

KIRBY #2

SPROAT #3/0
with weedguard

EAGLE CLAW

DOUBLE HOOK

TREBLE HOOK

**ABERDEEN** hook has round bend and wide gap. Of thin wire, it is popular live-bait hook for fresh water. Center hook has standard-length shank. Left hook is 2X short: #8 shank on #6 hook. Right hook is 2X long: #4 shank on #6 hook.

**KIRBY** has a round bend and a kirbed point—that is, offset to the left when hook is held shank down and point toward you. Point of a reversed hook is bent to the right. Offset in hook may speed hooking. Slices in shank help hold natural baits on hook.

**SPROAT** has a round bend much like Kirby except point is straight rather than offset. Bends slightly sharper than in usual round bends. Hook shown equipped with thin-wire weedguard to help prevent fouling.

**EAGLE CLAW** has a round bend, and the point is offset to right when hook is held shank down with point toward you. Point bends inward toward shank for fast penetration and good holding power. Available with slices in shank to hold bait.

**DOUBLE HOOKS** are made of single wire with shanks, bends, and points at each end. Hooks are at about 120-degree angle rather than directly opposed. Double hooks are used primarily for soft baits such as doughballs. Treble hooks, made by soldering a third hook to a double, ordinarily have shiny finish and add to flash of artificial lure.

**CARLISLE** has round bend, kirbed point, and long shank; commonly used for big baits. Hook shown above is snelled— that is, equipped with a length of leader. Some snelled hooks have gut leaders, others wire. Snelled hooks may be eyeless.

CARLISLE #5
snelled

**LIMERICK,** made of heavy wire, generally has straight point and an almost round bend. This varies with manufacturer, however. The Limerick is of Irish origin. Similar American design is Cincinnati Bass, which has a kirbed point and a round bend.

LIMERICK #1

**SHEEPSHEAD** hooks are made of heavy wire and have short shanks. Designed especially for sharp - toothed and gristly-mouthed salt-water fish.

SHEEPSHEAD #4

**SALMON EGG,** or Siwash, hooks have almost no shank but have extra-long points for deep, fast penetration in tough mouth.

SALMON EGG HOOK #4

**HUMPED SHANKS** are available for many hook styles. The crimps prevent turning of cork, rubber, or plastic body of artificial when fastened to long shank.

HUMPSHANK #7

**O'SHAUGHNESSY** style is usually made of heavy wire, forged to give the hook extra strength. Bend is round, and point is turned in. This is an all-around favorite for fresh and salt water. It is made of nickel, nickel alloy, or tinned steel. Size shown is for big fish.

O'SHAUGHNESSY #8/0

**OTHER METHODS** of fishing can be great fun and highly productive, though often considered to be less sporting than fishing with rod and reel. Some of these methods are especially suitable for taking kinds of fish, particularly rough fish, that cannot be caught easily with conventional tackle. Ice fishing equipment is for use in the northern winter season.

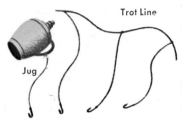

Trot Line

Jug

**TROT LINES** are heavy lines from which hang many baited hooks on short pieces of line. Strung between buoys or banks, trot lines are used principally for such fish as catfish in fresh water and cod in salt water. In jug fishing, each baited hook and line is tied to a floating jug or can, which holds hooked fish.

**BOWS and ARROWS** Tackle consists of simple reel that fastens above or below grip on bow. The reel holds 50 to 100 feet of strong, soft-braided nylon line. The line is tied to the arrow or to the point and slips from reel easily as arrow is shot. Points are barbed to hold fish.

**SPEARS and GIGS** are used from banks, bridges, and boats and by skin divers, who usually use a single-point spear with a metal shaft. It may be jabbed by hand or shot from rubber sling or compressed gas gun. Gigs, used from above water, have 3- or 5-prong heads and long handle.

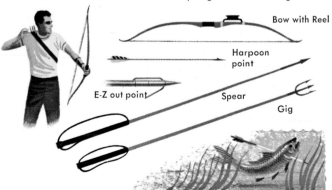

Bow with Reel

Harpoon point

E-Z out point

Spear

Gig

**ICE FISHING** probably produces more fish per value of tackle than any other method. Tools and tackle for ice fishing are simple and inexpensive. A spud, or ice chisel, is needed for cutting holes in the ice. This can be bought in a tackle shop or made by welding a carpenter's chisel to a length of iron pipe. (A hole cannot be shaped properly with an axe or a hatchet.) An ordinary kitchen strainer can be used as a skimmer to keep the hole open, but specially designed skimmers are manufactured. Automatic tip-ups are devices designed so that a fish raises a flag or rings a bell when it strikes. Tip-ups are most useful in live-bait fishing for pike, pickerel, and walleyes. Fishing sticks, which are like tiny rods, are excellent for use with spoons or with weighted ice flies, which are jigged up and down to attract such fish as perch, crappies, and bluegills. All natural baits are good for ice fishing. Crappies prefer live minnows.

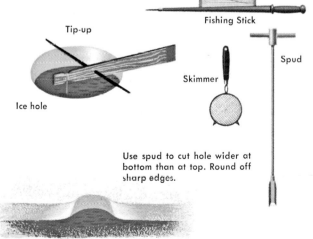

Fishing Stick

Tip-up

Spud

Skimmer

Ice hole

Use spud to cut hole wider at bottom than at top. Round off sharp edges.

**ACCESSORY TACKLE** helps indirectly in catching fish and may be very important. A sinker that holds the bait near the bottom in the tide, or the bobber (p. 108) that keeps the bait just off the bottom and indicates when a fish is biting—these are accessories that serve important functions. Swivels and snaps (p. 109) are also highly useful. Landing nets, gaffs, tackle boxes, bait buckets (pp. 110-111)—accessories of this type help less directly but add greatly to fishing success. Other accessories (pp. 112-113) add to the comfort and convenience of a fishing trip.

**SINKERS** are lead weights molded in various shapes and sizes. They are used mainly to keep a bait or lure at the desired level in the water, but in some cases their purpose is to provide weight for casting. Used in all types of fishing, sinkers should be just heavy enough to hold the bait where it is wanted.

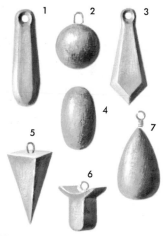

**BOTTOM-FISHING SINKERS** (Salt Water) The Bank Sinker (1) is an inexpensive good general-purpose sinker. It is usually tied below the hook, as are such other common types as the Round (2) and the Diamond-shaped (3). The Egg Sinker (4) slides on the line and works well for light-biting, wary fish; the fisherman can feel the slightest bite and the fish does not detect the weight. The Pyramid Sinker (5) is used in surf fishing on sandy bottoms. The Bulldozer (6) has great holding power in sand bottoms. The Dipsey (7), pear-shaped with swiveled brass center stem, good for surf fishing over rocky bottoms.

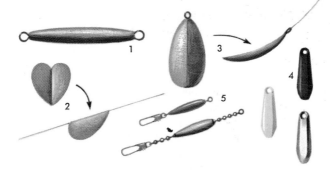

## TROLLING SINKERS

**TROLLING SINKERS** hold a bait or lure at the desired depth when trolling at a particular speed. In the conventional types (1) the line is fastened at one end and the leader at the other. The flat, heart-shaped style (2) folds over the line and forms a keel that helps to prevent the line from twisting.

## STILL-FISHING SINKERS

**STILL-FISHING SINKERS** (Fresh Water) The Adjustable Sinker (1) is attached to the line by means of coiled brass rings at each end of the sinker. Clinchers (2) are grooved and have ears that can be bent around the line to hold the sinker in place. Split-shot Sinkers (3) are fastened to the line similarly; like other sinkers, they come in a variety of sizes but are never large, ranging from BB size to large buckshot. The Gator Grip Sinker (4) is reusable, as are the Wraparound Sinkers (5), which are strips of lead ribbon that are wound around the line to give the desired weight. Dipseys (p. 106) are also used.

## SPECIAL PURPOSE SINKERS

**SPECIAL PURPOSE SINKERS** include the No-Snag type (3) that planes to the surface when retrieved rather than dragging along the bottom. Colored Bank Sinkers (4) help attract flounders and other kinds of fish. Casting Sinkers (5) are used ahead of light lures to give weight for easier casting.

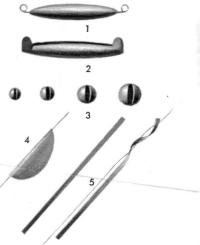

**BOBBERS,** or floats, are used mainly as indicators to tell when a fish is biting. They also hold baits at a desired level—out of the weeds and bottom debris or away from bottom-feeding fish—and some kinds are designed to attract fish. The simplest bobbers are made of unfinished cork or of a light wood, such as balsa. Many of the commercial bobbers are made of plastic and have patented devices to make it easy to fasten them on the line or to change their position. Brightly colored bobbers are easiest to see, most common being red and white.

**PLAIN CORKS** (1) may be slit to hold them on the line, or they can be bought with a center hole through which the line is threaded and then held in place with a stick (2). One of the most popular varieties is the Cork Ball (3). Egg Floats (4) are common, colorful commercial types, while the Quill Float (5) and the Pencil Float (6) are preferred for light-biting or suspicious fish, as they offer little resistance. Popping Corks (7) make a gurgling or popping noise when jerked and are used to attract game fish to the bait. Casting Floats (8) add weight for casting light lures or baits and are usually made to be filled with water to get the exact weight desired, as are Plastic Bubbles (9).

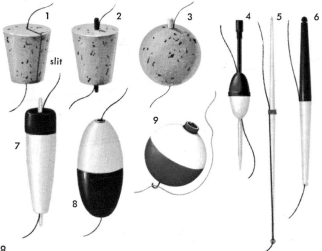

108

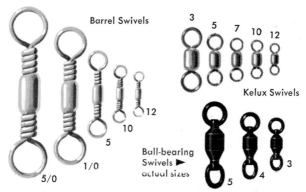

Barrel Swivels

Kelux Swivels

Ball-bearing
Swivels ►
actual sizes

**SWIVELS** permit a lure or bait to rotate without twisting the line and do not inhibit the action of the bait or lure. Barrel swivels consist of two loops of wire with their ends tucked inside a brass barrel. Very similar types, such as the Kelux, lack the twisted loops of wire exposed at the neck and have a cylindrical barrel. Ball-bearing swivels are carefully machined and rotate freely on stainless-steel ball bearings.

**SNAPS** provide a quick and convenient way to change hooks or lures. Safety snaps, which operate like a safety pin, are made of heavy stainless-steel wire and have a brass collar. Snap swivels consist of a snap at one end of a swivel and are often used when no leader is necessary.

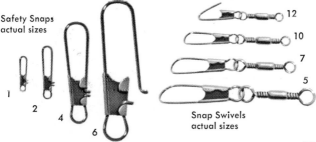

Safety Snaps
actual sizes

Snap Swivels
actual sizes

109

perforated inner lining

Minnow Bucket

Bait Box

Belt Bait Box

**BAIT CONTAINERS** of proper design are far superior to makeshift receptacles. The inner sections of minnow buckets are perforated so they drain quickly and make it easy to pick out the minnows. Worms can be kept alive for a long time in damp moss in insulated boxes with porous walls. Special worm or insect boxes that can be worn on the belt are especially useful when wading.

**TACKLE BOXES** keep lures, hooks and accessories in order. Tackle boxes may be made of metal, wood or plastic, and come in a wide range of sizes. Some are designed for use from boat, others for fishing from bank. Deep compartments keep dry-fly hackles from being crushed. In wet-fly boxes and in fly hooks, flies are carried flat.

Dry-fly Box

Wet-fly Box

Fly Book

Tackle Box
trays are in hinged tiers

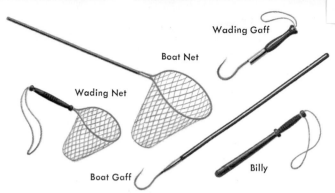

Wading Gaff

Boat Net

Wading Net

Boat Gaff

Billy

**GAFFS AND LANDING NETS** are used to help land played-out fish. Nets used by waders have a very short handle, often with a snap for fastening it to a ring or loop on the creel strap. Boat nets have a long handle of aluminum or wood. Gaffs, which are large barbless hooks on handles, are used for large fish. Billies are used to subdue large fish after landing.

**CREELS AND STRINGERS** keep the catch fresh and carry it conveniently. Creels, used mostly in trout fishing, are made of split willow, rattan, or canvas. A stringer may be a heavy cord with a needle at one end and a ring at the other. Better is chain type with individual snaps to hold fish through lips. Live bags are hung overboard.

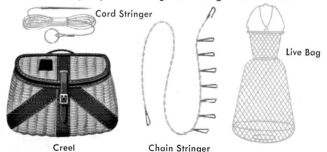

Cord Stringer

Live Bag

Creel

Chain Stringer

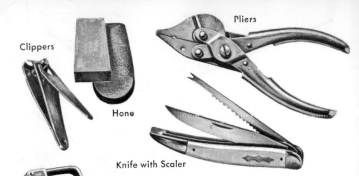

Clippers

Pliers

Hone

Knife with Scaler

DeLiar

Rod Holder

**TOOLS** of many kinds are useful to the fisherman; only the most important are shown here. Clippers, for cutting lines and leaders and for trimming knots; pliers with wire cutters, for making leaders and repairing tackle. A hone, to keep hooks and knife sharp; a knife for cutting bait and cleaning the catch. Unhooking a fish is easy with a disgorger. For trolling or still fishing, a rod holder leaves both hands free. DeLiar weighs and measures fish.

Floating Knife

Disgorger

**FLY-LINE DRESSING** helps keep a fly line smooth and waterproof. Dry Fly Oil must be used to keep flies floating.

**REEL OIL AND GREASE** prolong life of reel and also increase its smoothness of operation for casting and playing fish.

Dry Fly Oil

Line Dressing

Grease

Reel Oil

Vest

Jacket

Waders

Cap

Hip Boots

**CLOTHING** for the fisherman puts function ahead of style. The many pockets in a fisherman's vest or jacket hold lures, leaders and accessories. Hats and caps shade his eyes and protect his head from the beating sun. With boots and waders he can wade cold water in comfort. Wading shoes are worn over stocking foot waders. Polaroid glasses cut glare and enable fisherman to "read" the water and to see fish underwater.

Polaroid Glasses

Wading Shoes

**INSECT REPELLENTS** keep away the mosquitoes, gnats, sand flies, and chiggers that spoil many fishing trips.

**SUNTAN LOTIONS** protect face from sun's burning rays, intensified by reflection from water.

**KNOTS** that hold securely without slipping or seriously weakening the line are essential in fishing. The choice of the right knot is especially important with synthetic line and leader materials, both braided and monofilament, as they tend to slip easily and to weaken more than silk or linen when knotted. All the knots illustrated here are satisfactory for synthetics. Cut old knots and tie new ones from time to time when fishing, since all knots fray and weaken with use. In tying, always pull knots tight slowly and steadily; never with a jerk. Ends can be trimmed with clippers or singed with a match to form a bead of fused materials that helps to keep the knot from slipping.

**IMPROVED CLINCH KNOT** is used to tie lure, hook, or swivel to monofilament line or leader.

**LARK'S HEAD KNOT** uses Perfection Loop (p. 115) to attach swivels, hooks, or lures to line.

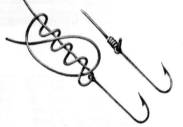

slip loop over lure and pull tight

**BLOOD KNOT** is best for joining pieces of monofilament of about the same diameter.

**DOUBLE SURGEON'S KNOT** is used to join lines of widely different diameters.

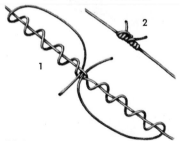

**NAIL KNOT** is used to join the butt of monofilament leader securely to the line.

**JAM KNOT** is used to attach fly line to a loop of monofilament or to a gut leader.

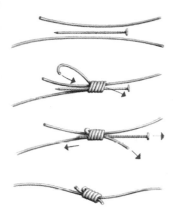

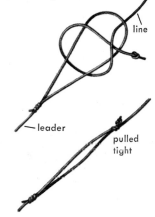

line

leader

pulled tight

**BIMINI TWIST KNOT** is used to make a secure, non-slip loop at the end of the line.

**PERFECTION LOOP** gives no "dog-leg" with monofilament, is strong with all line materials.

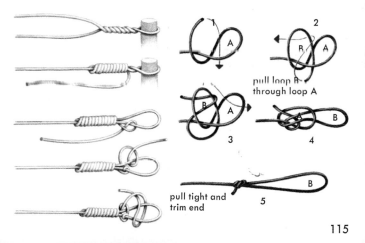

2

pull loop B through loop A

3

4

pull tight and trim end

5

**TERMINAL RIGS** present the bait or lure to the fish. Some are used to hold a bait where fish can see it or to keep it out of the reach of crabs or rough fish. Others allow a fish to run with the bait without feeling the sinker. Some are used to permit fishing more than one bait or lure at a time.

**BOTTOM RIGS** can be used either in fresh or in salt water. Illustrated are (1) a general-purpose two-hook rig; (2) a winter flounder rig, which is good also for other species; and (3) a sheepshead rig, with line feeding through egg sinker so weight does not bother wary fish.

**FISHFINDER RIGS** allow fish to take line without feeling the resistance of the sinker. They are especially useful in the surf but are also good in fresh water. Illustrated are a standard fishfinder rig (4) and a fishfinder rig with a cork ball (5) that keeps bait off the bottom.

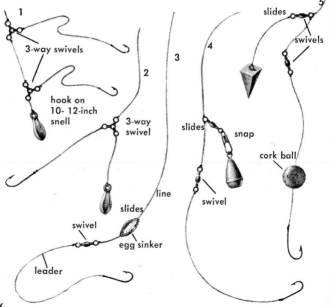

1
3-way swivels

hook on 10- 12-inch snell

2
3-way swivel

3

4
slides
snap

slides

swivel

line

slides
egg sinker

swivel

leader

5
slides
swivels

cork ball

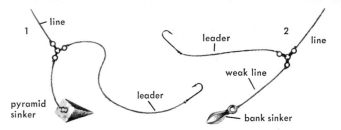

## SURF RIGS

On sand beaches a pyramid sinker (1) holds best. In rocks, bank sinker (2) or dipsey is tied to a weak piece of line below the hook. When a hang-up occurs, sinker breaks off easily.

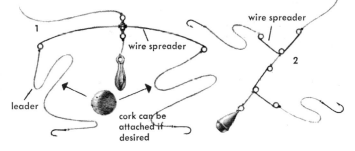

## SPREADER RIGS

(above) use stainless steel or bronze spreaders to keep hooks apart at same level (1) or to hold hooks out from line (2). Corks may be used to keep baits off bottom.

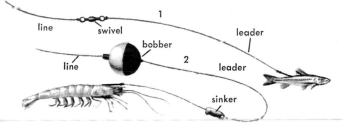

## LIVE-LINE RIGS

(above) present live baits naturally. Leader may be connected to the line at swivel (1), or in another type (2) plastic float and clincher sinker are used on monofilament line.

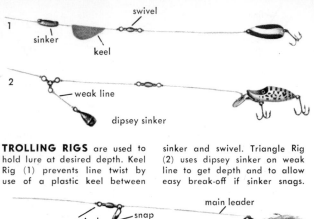

**TROLLING RIGS** are used to hold lure at desired depth. Keel Rig (1) prevents line twist by use of a plastic keel between sinker and swivel. Triangle Rig (2) uses dipsey sinker on weak line to get depth and to allow easy break-off if sinker snags.

**DOUBLE-JIG RIG** (above) is made by attaching snap of trailing leader through lower swivel eye of main leader.

**SPLASHER-JIG RIGS** attract fish by sound. Dowel (1) or a popping cork (2) may be attached between line and leader.

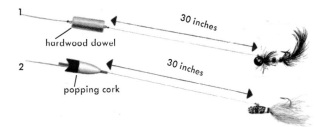

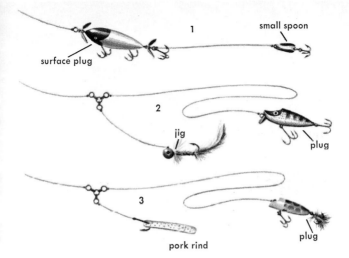

surface plug

small spoon

1

2

jig

plug

3

pork rind

plug

**COMBINATION RIGS** offer fish a choice of two lures. Three popular combinations are: (1) a surface plug trailed by a small spoon, excellent for White Bass; (2) feather jig and plug rig, good for many fresh- and salt-water game fish; (3) pork rind strip and plug combination, a favorite for Striped Bass in surf.

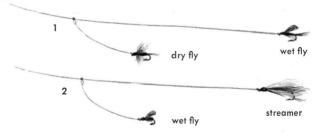

1

dry fly

wet fly

2

wet fly

streamer

**DROPPER FLY RIGS** are popular in trout fishing. Shown are (1) a dry-fly dropper that serves as an indicator, or "bobber," for wet fly or nymph, (2) streamer fly with a wet-fly dropper.

## WHERE, WHEN, AND HOW TO FISH

A good fisherman can fish different types of water with success. He knows how to read water conditions and understands the habits of fish. This knowledge is as important for catching fish as an understanding of tackle and how to use it.

**WHY FISH BITE**   Fish are opportunists. If conditions suit them, they generally feed whenever food is available. A hatch of insects on a stream brings the trout out of hiding. A school of minnows stirs the appetites of bass or mackerel. Sometimes, often in competition with others of their kind, fish will continue to eat until they are too full to swallow more. Again, they may refuse food for long periods, even when it is dangled in front of them.

The temperature of the water has a direct bearing on a fish's hunger and activity. If the water temperature is too low, fish become inactive. As the water temperature climbs, its dissolved oxygen content decreases, and again the fish become less active. Somewhere between these extremes is a temperature range that fish seek, and it differs with each species. Largemouth Bass are most active when the water temperature is between 65 and 75 degrees F.; Smallmouth Bass prefer slightly cooler water—60 to 70 degrees F. For Brook Trout, the best temperature is from 50 to 65 degrees F. Lake Trout are most active in water in the low 40's. In fishing deep lakes, some fishermen lower thermometers to measure the temperature of the water at various levels, then put their bait or lures at the proper depth for the fish they are after.

Tides and currents bring food to fish. Game fish feed where strong currents keep bait fish, shrimp, and other food animals stirred up. Salt-water fish look for food on the turn of the tide, as the reversed flow of water uncovers hiding food animals. Most fishermen favor the incoming (flood) tide, but the outgoing (ebb) tide may be as good or better, particularly in its early stages when the bait is most disturbed (pp. 136-137). Likewise, in fresh water, small streams entering larger streams or lakes may carry food and are likely places to find fish feeding. Except as it is related to tides, the moon has no direct effect on fish activity.

In both fresh and salt water, fish that find their food by sight prefer clear water; scent and taste feeders are more active at night or in murky water. All fish stop feeding, at least temporarily, when frightened. Most fish seem to feed sparingly during unsettled weather conditions. It seems generally true that fish feed more actively when the barometer is rising than when it is falling, but the availability of food and the temperature of the water are more important. Calendars cannot make accurate predictions of good fishing days with any more reliability than they can predict the weather.

**FISHING METHODS** Most of the methods described here are useful in both fresh and salt water and will work equally well with different kinds of tackle. A few were developed for a particular type of water or kind of fish. For rigs, see pp. 116-119.

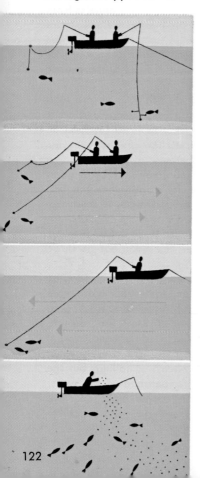

**STILL FISHING,** with natural baits and with hand line, cane pole, or rod and reel, may be done from shore, bridge, pier, or anchored boat. The bait may be fished on the bottom or held off bottom by a float. The bait is allowed to remain more or less still until a fish bites.

**DRIFT FISHING** is done by trailing the line behind a drifting boat. The line may be unweighted, weighted to reach the bottom, or held at a desired level in the water by attaching a float. Natural baits are best for drift fishing, but jigged artificials are also good (p. 123).

**LIVE LINING,** most effective in tideways and flowing streams, is a method in which natural baits are allowed to drift with the current over and through "holes" where fish lie. Usually, no sinker is used, but the bait may be held at a desired level in the water by attaching a float.

**CHUMMING** is a means of attracting fish by throwing quantities of ground-up bait (chum) into the water from shore or from a boat, or by stirring natural foods from bottom with a rake. Chumming puts fish in a feeding mood and helps them to overcome their natural caution.

**TROLLING** is usually done by trailing an artificial or natural bait behind a moving boat. Trolling speed and the depth of bait or lure are varied with the kind of fish being sought. Towing a bait or lure while walking along a bridge or pier is also trolling (see Trolling Rigs, p. 118).

**MOOCHING,** a modified type of trolling, is used in fishing for Pacific Salmon. The bait is sunk deep with a heavy sinker, then brought upward at an angle as the boat is run forward a few yards. The boat is stopped and the bait sinks. This raising and lowering is repeated often.

**JIGGING** is done by jerking a lure straight upward, then letting it fall back again. The lure is kept in almost continuous motion, and fish usually strike as jig is on rise. Jigs (p. 70) were developed to be used in this manner. Jigging is used in fresh or salt water, also in ice fishing.

**BOTTOM BOUNCING** is a type of jigging in which the lure or sinker is allowed to bump the bottom and raise a puff of sand or mud. This method is very effective with bucktail jigs and also works well in bottom fishing with natural baits. The commotion stirs fish to strike.

123

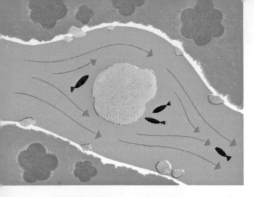

A boulder in midstream splits current, creating a quiet spot with a turbulent area behind it. Fish can rest in calm spot, feed in cross-currents below.

**STREAMS** offer a changing variety of feeding stations for fish. In all streams, there are stretches where fish are plentiful and others in which there are few or no fish. Finding the most productive spots is simply a matter of "reading" the stream to discover where the fish will be found when feeding and where they rest.

A fast stream usually has some deep pools, riffles, flats, eddies, backwaters, rapids, and perhaps even waterfalls. Trout and salmon are the principal game fish of fast, cold streams. When feeding, trout may lie in the main current, in the deep water just over drop-offs or behind boulders where the current is slowed. Smallmouth Bass, Walleyes,

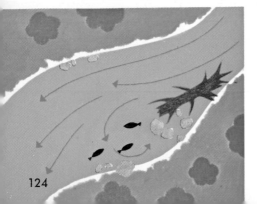

Log jams or rocks against one bank may cause an eddy on the downstream side. Eddies hold and concentrate food and provide easy feeding for fish.

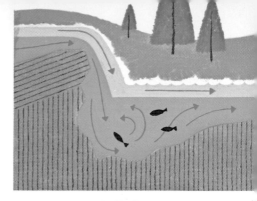

Fish often concentrate below waterfalls because they can't get past them. Churned water below falls is rich in oxygen, making fish active.

and panfish are common in warmer but still cool streams. Fish are generally found where they can feed comfortably and safely. Bass and Walleyes usually stay in deep eddies or in large pools but commonly move into the riffles at the head of a pool to feed in early morning or at dusk. This is especially true in midsummer, when the fish tend to stay in deep or shaded water during the heat of the day. It the water becomes very warm, fish may feed only at night. Fish of fast streams are highly cautious and keep hidden when not feeding. When a supply of food brings them out of hiding, they become less wary, but still they demand careful fishing.

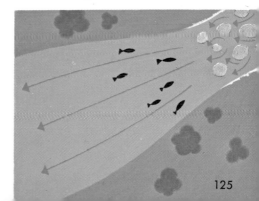

Riffles are stretches of fast, slightly turbulent shallow water, often leading into pools. Fish feed where riffles tumble food into slower water of pools.

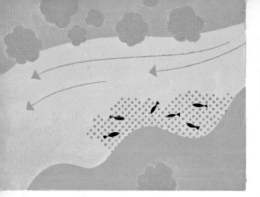

One shore is often fairly deep, with brush or trees shading the water. Opposite shore, if ill-defined, shallow, and weedy, makes good feeding grounds.

Slow streams usually meander. At bends, there are deep holes and undercut banks. Often there are lily pads, water weeds, or scrub thickets along the banks, and sometimes trees shade the shore line. In wide, deep stretches, the water may be nearly still; where the stream narrows, there may be a strong current. The principal fish of slow fresh-water streams are Largemouth Bass, Muskellunge, pickerels, catfish, and panfish. Snook, Tarpon, Striped Bass, and weakfish are often found in slow tidal streams.

Bends are among the best spots to fish in slow streams. Here the fish get both food and cover in the deep holes and undercut banks. Schooling panfish congregate along

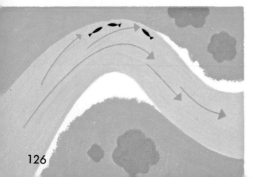

Bends have deep holes and undercut banks along their outer sides where fish congregate. The inside of a bend is usually shallow, often with a sand bar.

126

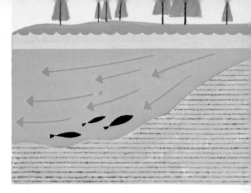

A drop-off in stream bottom, where the deep water is downstream from the shallow, is a natural spot for fish to lie in wait for food.

the outer edge of such bends. Bass, Muskellunge and pickerel frequently feed in the weedy stretches of shore line or at the mouths of smaller feeder streams, where baitfish are often plentiful. In tidal creeks, feeder streams are especially good on the falling tide, when the flow carries food into the main stream.

Streams change quickly; swift streams are altered in character more rapidly than slow streams. Loads of sand and silt are deposited by flood waters, when currents cut new channels and create new bends, pools, and rapids. Most streams must be studied again each season to find the most productive spots to fish.

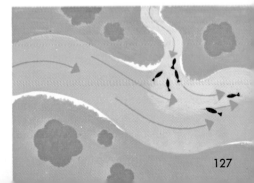

Feeder creeks entering the main stream carry baitfish and other food to hungry game fish. Such spots are excellent in tidal estuaries on outgoing tide.

127

Pickerel in weed bed.

Bass in shade of lily pads.

Crappie in brush pile.

Feeder stream brings food.

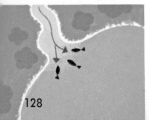

## PONDS AND SHALLOW LAKES

are usually good fishing waters. Plants grow in abundance in rich, shallow waters and in turn support a large population of fish and smaller animals on which they feed. In warm to moderately cool ponds and lakes, the typical fish are Northern Pike, Largemouth Bass, Smallmouth Bass, Walleyes, Yellow Perch, Bluegills, pickerels, crappies, bullheads, and many of the smaller panfish. Cold-water lakes and ponds in the mountains or in the North may also yield Brook, Brown, Rainbow or other trouts.

Both game fish and panfish feed along the shore line and where there are weeds or other cover for the food animals and for the smaller fish to hide from the larger fish. Open water at the edge of weed beds can be fished with natural baits and with most artificials. Weedless lures can be worked right through the weeds without fouling. Surface lures will ride over the top of submerged weeds. Shore lines of lakes are fished most effectively by casting lures from a boat toward the shore. Small ponds can be fished from the bank, and sometimes the lure or bait can be worked from shore to shore.

Weedless lures are especially [use]ful in shallow lakes, where [fish] commonly feed and rest in we[eds] and snag-filled areas (see p. [...]

Deep, cool pockets ar[e good] in summer, when the wat[er is warm] from top to bottom. Fish [may be] shaded by overhanging [trees or] lily pads spread over th[e surface. Fish] congregate where feede[r streams enter a stream] or lake. Here the water i[s cooler in summer and warmer] in winter and is usually richer with food carried in by the current. Brush piles, fallen trees, old docks, or other objects under the water are favorite lairs of game fish, as are the stump- and snag-filled areas common in man-made lakes. Shoals extending out from shore and bordered by drop-offs to deeper water are also choice feeding grounds and productive fishing spots.

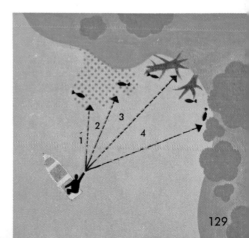

In fishing a shallow lake, keep your boat well out from shore. First make short casts (1 and 2) to weed beds or shoals. Then make longer casts to reach the shore lines and close-in cover (3 and 4).

129

**DEEP LAKES** provide fish with the same sorts of food and cover situations as do ponds and shallow lakes (p. 128), but because a large, deep lake covers a great area, its best fishing spots may be harder to find. In addition to the kinds of fish found in ponds and shallow lakes, such species as Landlocked Salmon, Lake Trout, and Muskellunge, which need more space or colder water, may be found in these larger bodies of water.

As in ponds, shallow lakes, and streams, fish are most abundant near edges, where two or more types of habitat meet and thus furnish food and cover all in one spot. The most continuous edge is the shore line, some parts of which are more productive than others. Best are sharply sloping banks or places providing rocks, logs, brush, or trees as cover for fish. Also good are shady coves, weed beds, rock ledges, or bars that stretch out from points of land and create shoals where fish feed.

Large, deep lakes change in character with the season. Before a lake freezes in winter, the water throughout the lake cools to 39.2 degrees F., the temperature at which water is heaviest. When water becomes colder than 39.2 degrees F., it becomes lighter and no longer sinks. Finally —at 32 degrees F.—it turns to ice, which literally floats on the top. In winter, most of the fish in the lake seek the deepest level at which they can find sufficient oxygen for their survival; this happens also to be the warmest water. Some fish, such as Chain Pickerel, Walleyes, and Yellow Perch, continue to feed actively even under the ice and are caught by ice fishing methods (p. 105).

When the ice melts in spring, the water first becomes

In winter, a lake freezes over after surface temperature of water drops below 32°F. Most fish become inactive and stay in deep water where it is warmer. Yellow Perch and a few other kinds continue to feed and provide sport for ice fishermen.

When the ice melts in spring, the temperature of water becomes the same throughout the lake for a brief period. All the fish then feed at the surface or in the shallows where the water is richest in oxygen and contains an abundance of food.

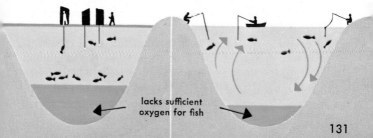

lacks sufficient oxygen for fish

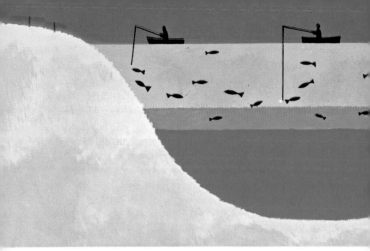

warmed and heavier. It sinks and is replaced by colder, lighter water from below. The lake is said to "turn" as the water circulates from top to bottom. For a brief time in early spring all the water in the lake is at about the same temperature, but because the wave-whipped water at the surface is richest in oxygen and food, all fish, including the cold-water species such as trout, feed at the surface.

Summer brings about still another change in the lake. Warmed by the sun, the water at the surface rises above 39.2 degrees F. and becomes lighter than the water beneath. The mixing stops, and soon the lake is divided into three temperature layers. In the top layer, the water is warm and has an adequate supply of oxygen churned in from the surface. Almost all of the fish in the lake can be found in this layer. In the thin middle layer, the temperature drops sharply. Fish cannot live in the bottom layer, where the water is very cold—close to 39.2 degrees F. throughout—and there is little or no food or oxygen. By the end of summer, the top layer may have become very

In summer, the surface water warms to well above 39.2°F. and floats on the heavier water below. Mixing ceases, and lake stratifies into 3 layers. Fish are found in warm top layer, which is rich in oxygen, and a few in or near the middle layer, a zone of rapidly descending temperature. The bottom layer is cold and low in oxygen.

thick, from 35 to as much as 60 or 70 feet depending on the location and depth of the lake.

While the lake's water is stratified in the warm months, fish seek the temperature level at which they are most comfortable. Largemouth Bass, Northern Pike, and other fish of warm to cool water are found close to the surface and in the shallows. Trout and other cold-water fish stay in deep water, usually close to or in the middle layer. To catch these fish in summer, a fisherman must drop his baits or lures deep. For either trolling or still fishing at depths of 50 or 60 feet, a wire line is needed (see trolling rigs, pp. 118-119). To determine the proper depth to fish, a thermometer can be lowered into the water to find the zone where the temperature drops suddenly.

In autumn the lake "turns" again as the surface water cools and sinks and the warmer water from the bottom rises. As in spring, the mixing of water results in a period when the lake has a uniform temperature from top to bottom, and cold-water species again feed at the surface.

**PIERS** provide fishermen with access to deep water and also furnish cover for fish. A pier that juts out from a sand beach may be the only shelter in miles. Piers commonly shelter schools of bait fish that attract passing schools of Bluefish, Pollock, mackerels, and other game fish. Mussels or barnacles encrusted on the piling entice such fish as Sheepshead, Tautogs and porgies. In fresh water, piers are fine for Yellow Perch, crappies, and other panfish.

The deep end of a pier is not always best, however, for fish feed near shore at times, especially when breaking waves keep food animals stirred up. Night fishing is popular, for game fish come to feed on the bait fish attracted to lights. Bottom fishing with natural baits and casting with artificials are both good.

Fish too large to lift on line or leader can be landed by drop net.

Among the giants caught from piers and bridges is the jewfish.

**BRIDGES** spanning fresh-water streams are especially good spots for panfish and catfish. Over salt water, they are favorite haunts of such shade-lovers as Sheephead, Tautogs, and many kinds of snappers and grunts. Blue-fish, mackerels, weakfish, croakers, and other roamers pass under bridges regularly as they follow the tide flow to feed. On moonlit nights such game fish as Snook, Tarpon, and Striped Bass gather on the uptide side of the bridge to prey on shrimp, minnows, and other bait animals that congregate just in front of the bridge's shadow. This is a productive spot to fish with such artificial lures as bucktails and metal jigs. In bottom fishing with natural baits, let the current carry the bait beneath the bridge if fishing for the shade lovers. Or let the bait drift out from the bridge if you are after tide-following game fish. Causeways to bridges are also considered good fishing spots.

Live lining and bottom fishing are best on the downtide side.

Night casting is best on uptide side, where bait fish concentrate.

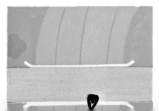

135

**BAYS AND LAGOONS,** connected to the open sea by inlets or passes, are ideal for the small-boat fisherman. He can troll, drift fish, or drop anchor in a productive spot and either bottom fish or cast.

Some kinds of fish range in and out of bays with the tide; others spend their life in these relatively quiet waters. But most fish caught in bays are seasonal residents. In winter they migrate to deeper, warmer offshore waters or move southward. Among the common fish caught in the bays and lagoons of the Atlantic and Gulf coasts are Striped Bass, Tautogs, Bluefish, Pompano, Snook, Tarpon, groupers, croakers, and flounders. Popular bay fish of the Pacific are Chinook Salmon, kelp basses, rockfishes, croakers, groupers, and flatfish.

In bays, as in other waters, fish concentrate where they find food or cover. Bare bottom areas are poor places to fish. On an incoming tide, many fish gather just inside the inlets, especially where a current forms an eddy that holds the food animals. On the outgoing tide, the fish move through the pass and feed outside at the edges of bars and in eddies. Flats along shore and in coves are best near high tide, when fish range into the shallows to

A. Incoming (flood) tide: food animals stirred up; fish feeding.
B. Slack tide: no current; food animals not active.
C. Outgoing (ebb) tide: food animals stirred up; fish feeding.

**TROLL** by running the boat against tide, towing bait or lure behind. Speed of boat usually hooks fish when it hits. When fish are located, boat can be anchored for casting or bottom fishing.

**DRIFT** with the tide. Boat moves slowly, so give fish line and allow it to swallow bait before setting hook. If casting, cast into or across tide and let current carry bait or lure.

feed. Steep shores are most productive on a high, falling tide. Channels are usually best at low tide, when fish leave the flats. Oyster or mussel beds, in water from 3 to 12 feet deep, are feeding grounds usually good on any tide, as are the kelp beds along the West Coast. Grass flats, where the water is from 4 to 6 feet deep, also attract many kinds of bay fish, as do rocky bottoms. Where fish lack cover and feeding grounds, artificial reefs are created by sinking wrecked automobiles, concrete-weighted crates or other objects. These spots are usually marked with buoys to make them easy to find.

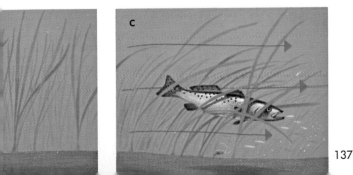

**SURF FISHING** is almost always best in early morning, late evening, or after dark. On sand beaches, fish are rarely active during the bright part of the day because the beach offers virtually no cover.

Striped Bass, Red Drum, Bluefish, California Corbina, Florida Pompano, surfperches, croakers, kingfish, and weakfishes are common surf catches. Most of these fish like to lie just beyond the bars or in the inshore sloughs where they can catch the food stirred up by breaking waves. Bars located off the beaches cause swells to steepen sharply, then break. Inshore sloughs can be located by a flattening of the waves and by the slightly darker color of the water. A natural cut through a bar leading into a slough is an outstanding spot. Special tackle for surf fishing is described on pp. 92-95.

In sandy surfs, fish congregate in sloughs and along the drop-off beyond the outside bar.

**ROCKY SHORES AND JETTIES** may provide good fishing all day long, as the fish have enough cover in the rocks nearby to feel safe while feeding. From a jetty, a fisherman can easily fish bars and holes unreachable from shore. Using either natural or artificial baits, he can cast or bottom fish with any kind of tackle.

In fresh water, jetties are good spots for Largemouth Bass, Smallmouth Bass, White Bass, Yellow Perch, catfish and many panfish. In salt water, jetties and rocky shores attract all of the common surf fishes as well as Tautog, Sheepshead, rockfishes, and others that seek cover regularly. Jetties create strong eddies by diverting the tide's flow, forming deep holes and feeding spots for fish. Many fish congregate where jetties are broken, allowing the tide to flow through.

Jetties furnish cover for fish and also alter currents to cause eddies and tide rips.

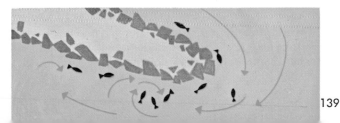

139

Fishing from stern is best, but everybody is busy when fish hit.

**PARTY BOATS** operate on regular schedules taking fishermen to offshore fishing grounds. Because anyone who wants to fish can get aboard as long as space is available, these boats are called Open Boats in some localities. Or because there is charge per person or head, they may be referred to as Head Boats. Depending on the area, the length of the trip, and the type of fishing, party-boat fees range from $15.00 to $40.00, usually including bait. Some boats stay out all day; others make two trips. Some specialize in night fishing or in fishing for only one species. In the upper Gulf region, many of the party boats fish only for Red Snappers in extremely deep water.

The typical party boat is fairly large, with a broad beam and a wide stern. A rail runs completely around the gunwales. The best spot is at the stern. Here you are closer to the water for easier fishing and a smoother ride, and you have less chance of tangling lines with fellow fishermen. But to get the stern position, be at the dock well ahead of sailing time.

On a good day nearly every fisherman on a party boat trip catches fish.

West Coast party boats generally use sardines or anchovies for bait, carrying them alive in large tanks. At the fishing grounds, scoops of these bait fish are tossed into the water for chum. As soon as fish begin to strike, the fishermen drop their baited hooks overboard, letting their unweighted lines ride the current with the chum. Yellowtail, Albacore, Bluefin Tuna, and Pacific Barracuda are commonly caught from these party boats.

In the Atlantic and Gulf of Mexico, party boats usually fish the bottom, either by anchoring or by slow drifting. Principal baits are clams, menhaden, cut mullet, and ballyhoo. Cod, Pollock, Black Sea Bass, Silver Hake, King Mackerel, Warsaw Grouper, flounders, snappers, porgies, groupers, and grunts are common catches.

On some party boats tackle is furnished or may be rented, but it is best to bring your own. Heavy spinning gear is a favorite among party-boat fishermen. Long, flexible boat rods equipped with salt-water reels are used also. A line of at least 30-pound test is needed for hauling the fish aboard.

Charter boats specialize in big-game fishing in offshore waters.

**CHARTER BOATS** are hired by one or several fishermen for a particular kind of fishing. The smaller of two general types is the guide boat, which may be a canoe, a johnboat for drifting a river, or a small, fast runabout. Seldom do more than two people fish from a guide boat, and the fishing is usually done with bait casting, fly casting, or spinning tackle. The operator of a guide boat serves also as a guide, and if you are unfamiliar with the area and have limited time to learn the water, he is

The flat-bottomed johnboat is a good guide boat for river float fishing.

well worth his price. The cost of chartering a guide boat ranges from a minimum of $30.00 a day for trout fishing in the North Country or for bass fishing in the Ozarks to as much as $150.00 a day for Bonefish or Tarpon in southern Florida or for salmon fishing in the Northwest. Guide boats can also be hired for Striped Bass, Red Drum, Snook, Northern Pike, Largemouth Bass, and others.

Larger charter boats for offshore ocean fishing range in length from 20 to more than 40 feet. They are equipped with outriggers for trolling and with fishing chairs for fighting heavy game fish. Most charter boats carry all the tackle needed for big-game fishing, and its use is included in the fee. Charter boat prices range from $100 to $500 or more a day, depending on location and season. This cost can be shared by 4 to 6 fishermen. Charter boats specialize in Sailfish, Marlin, Swordfish, Bluefin Tuna, Wahoo, King Mackerel, Dolphin, Amberjacks, Tarpon, and other big-game species. The usual methods are trolling or drifting. A mate prepares the baits, rigs the lines, and gaffs the catch; the skipper runs the boat.

Outriggers are used for trolling baits on or near the surface behind the charter boat. Made of bamboo, fiberglass, or aluminum, and 20 to 40 feet long, they are held at a 45-degree angle for fishing. The fishing line is attached to the outrigger by a snap clothespin, which releases on a strike (p. 18).

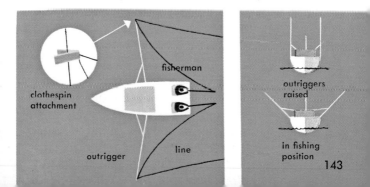

clothespin attachment

fisherman

outrigger

line

outriggers raised

in fishing position

143

**HOOKING A FISH** is basically a matter of jerking the line at the right instant to set the point of the hook in the fish's mouth. In fishing with natural baits, it is generally best to wait until the fish runs with the bait before attempting to set the hook. With soft baits, like doughballs (p. 62) or clams (p. 65), try to set the hook more quickly, for these baits are easily stolen. Proper timing for setting the hook comes only with experience. With artificial lures, the hook should be set the instant a strike is felt. Fishermen often try to set the hook too soon with artificials because they see the fish or hear it splash before it actually takes the lure.

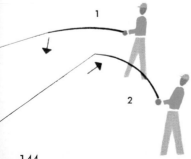

**BEFORE SETTING HOOK,** lower the rod (1) to allow more leverage. If using large live baits, first let fish take several feet of line from the reel.

Strike firmly, thumbing reel spool or holding the handle as the rod is snapped to a vertical position (2). You are now ready to play the fish (p. 145).

**PLAYING A FISH** provides much of the fun of fishing; it is the technique of keeping a fish hooked and tiring it out. The rod does the main job; it absorbs sudden jolts and applies relentless pressure on the fish. The rod does its job best when it is kept at a right angle to the fish's pull (1). If the fish makes a fast or a long run, lower the rod tip immediately (2) to reduce friction of the line on guides. Allow a running fish to strip line almost directly from the reel, with little bend in the rod.

**WHEN FISH STOPS,** pump it back with the rod (not by cranking the reel). This prevents breaking the line and possible damage to reel gears if the fish makes a sudden strong lunge. In pumping, bring the rod upward (3) to pull fish toward you. Then lower the rod rapidly toward the fish (4) and at the same time reel in the slack line. Be ready to stop pumping the moment the fish starts running or jumping again. Pumping should be done only to work the fish in during lulls in its fight.

**FISH IS IN LANDING POSITION** when it is within a rod's length or slightly more distant. (If fish is brought closer, landing it is made awkward, and there is a chance of breaking the rod.) Lean forward and hold the rod behind you (5) as you get ready to land catch (p. 146).

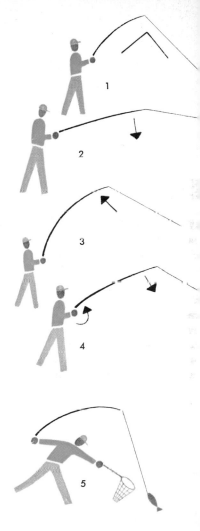

**LANDING** After a fish has been fully played-out, it can be landed by hand, net, or gaff—or small fish may simply be lifted in with the line. Fish escape while being landed usually because a fisherman becomes excited and tries to hurry.

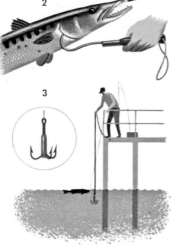

**NET FISH** head first (1). In trying to escape, fish will dive right into the net. With a sharp gaff, fish can be hooked anywhere in the body, but it is best to gaff it either in the gills (2) or under the lower jaw. Fish gaffed in the jaw will live if released. Played-out fish can be landed from bridges with a drop net (p. 134), or with a "snatch hook," which is in effect a gaff on a heavy cord (3). Fresh-water bass or other fish without large teeth can be landed by thrusting thumb into fish's mouth and gripping the lower jaw (4). This stuns fish and stops its struggles. Pikes and other fish with teeth can be stunned and lifted from water by gripping with thumb and second finger in eyesockets (5).

# CARE OF THE CATCH

Ideally, fish should be cleaned and cooked immediately after they are caught. As this is rarely practical, they should either be kept alive, which is most desirable, or be kept cool and moist until they can be cleaned.

**KEEP FISH ALIVE** in water on a snap-type stringer, in a live bag (p. 111), or in a boat's live well (p. 154). If fish cannot be kept alive and several hours will pass before they can be cleaned, remove their gills and entrails to prevent spoilage. A creel (p. 111) lined with damp leaves, grass, or cloth will keep catch cool and moist. Ice chests will keep the catch when fishing from a boat or the bank. Wet burlap bags are good in cool weather. Surf fishermen sometimes bury their fish in damp sand. Kill soon after landing.

If ready to be killed, a sharp rap on the head with a billy (p. 111) kills fish and, in the case of large ones, eliminates the danger of having them thrash about in the boat.

**TO RELEASE** an unwanted fish alive, handle it gently and as little as possible. If hook is too deep to be removed without damaging fish, cut it off between eye and bend or cut the leader. Fish will absorb the hook in time. To revive a played-out fish, hold it head forward in current or move it through water.

current

Surf fisherman may bury catch in the sand.

Scaler

Filleting Knife

Fish Brush

**CLEANING FISH**  Fish are easier to scale or to skin if worked on while fresh. A bench or a table, running water, and a sharp knife help make the job easier. The most important tool is the filleting knife, made of good steel and with a long, thin blade. A scaler is inexpensive, and a brush can be used to scrub out clotted blood from along backbone inside the body cavity. The method of cleaning varies with the kind of fish and how it is to be cooked. Consult a good cook book on how to cook fish.

**SCALE FISH,** unless it is to be filleted and skinned (p. 149). Hold fish by the tail and then scrape from tail to head to loosen and remove scales. Use a fish scaler or a dull knife. Cut off head behind pectoral fins.

**REMOVE FINS** of panfish by cutting into flesh on both sides of each fin (1. Pull out fins, bones and all. (Never clip fins, as this leaves small, sharp bones. Also may cut off tail (2).

1

2

**FILLETING** is easiest to do with fish over a foot long. First cut off head close behind pectoral fins (1), and then slit the belly to the vent (2). Remove entrails and wash out the abdominal cavity, using brush if necessary (3). Some prefer to fillet fish without steps 1, 2, and 3. Start knife alongside backbone and hold it flat as fillet is cut off (4). Turn fish over and cut fillet from other side. Fins stay on backbone (5), leaving two boneless fillets.

**TO SKIN,** lay fillet skin side down on flat surface (6), and start fillet knife under skin at tail end. Hold skin with fingers as it is cut from fillet. To remove few remaining bones, cut off rib cage as shown by dotted line (7).

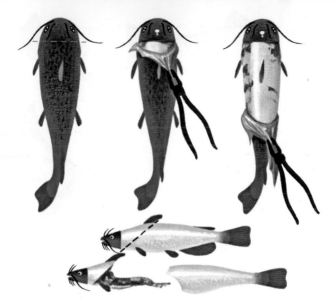

**TO SKIN CATFISH,** dip fish in hot water for a few seconds to loosen the skin. Cut through the skin all the way around head (1). Pull skin back with pliers (2 and 3). Head can be nailed to a board or held with another pair of pliers as the skin is pulled off. Cut through the backbone behind the dorsal fin on an angle toward the head (4). Break the head downward from the body, thus removing head and entrails at the same time (5).

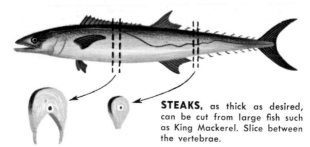

**STEAKS,** as thick as desired, can be cut from large fish such as King Mackerel. Slice between the vertebrae.

**TROPHY FISH** are extra large, unusual, or otherwise noteworthy catches made into durable, lifelike mounts by a taxidermist. Keep the fish cool and moist until it can be taken to a taxidermist. If the fish is too large to fit into an ice chest, wrap it in wet cloths; do not gut it. Before it is put away, measure its length in a straight line from the tip of its jaw to the tip of its tail. Do not let the tape follow the contour of the fish. Measure its girth in the thickest part of its body.

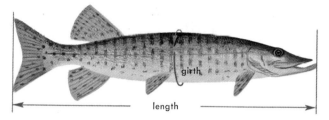

girth

length

**RECORDS** If you think you may have caught a record fish, measure it as shown above and also have it weighed on government inspected scales—do both in the presence of two witnesses. Photograph your fish whenever possible. For a fresh-water fish registration form, write to National Fresh Water Fishing Hall of Fame, Box 33, Hall of Fame Drive, Hayward, WI 54843, where over-all records for fresh-water fish are kept. For salt-water fish, write to International Game Fish Association (3000 E. Las Olas Blvd., Ft. Lauderdale, FL 33316) to get entry form, tackle rules, and a list of the current records. Your fish may be a record for the line test you used even if it is not an all-tackle record. The International Spin Fishing Association (P.O. Box 81, Downey, CA 90241) compiles records for fish caught on spinning tackle in both fresh and salt water. Here, too, your fish may qualify for a record for a particular line test.

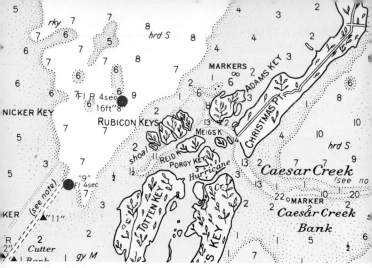

**NAVIGATION CHARTS** are considered basic equipment by salt-water fishermen. The best are the Coast, Harbor, and Small Craft charts, which show water depths at mean low tide, average tide range, contours of all shore lines, type of bottom, and locations of channels, bars, and tide rips. With these charts, a fisherman can find exactly the type bottom and water depth preferred by the fish he is after. Depending on the type of chart, its size, and the area covered, the cost ranges from one to several dollars. Charts can be purchased at bookstores and marinas or directly from the U.S. Coast and Geodetic Survey in Washington, D.C. For fresh water, topographic maps, available from the Geological Survey, Reston, Virginia, may be helpful in finding feeder streams, springs, and fishable shore lines of lakes. Locally prepared maps distributed at fishing camps or by chambers of commerce in most popular fishing areas are also helpful in learning new waters.

**FISH CONSERVATION** provides good fishing today and for the future. The size and bag limits of fish management programs are designed to utilize fish wisely as a renewable natural resource.

Fishermen should learn what is being done to maintain the good fishing in their areas and also how it can be made better. The fish conservation programs of state and national government agencies are paid for with the money fishermen pay for fishing licenses and also with the federal tax money collected on the sale of fishing tackle. Most of the money is used to buy public rights-of-way to existing waters, to build new lakes, for stocking fish, and for research programs to learn more about fish. Much more research needs to be done—and particularly on salt water fishes. As more is learned about fish through research, the fishing can be made better. For example, in some areas and for some kinds of fish it may be good conservation to keep what you catch; in others it may be wise to release catches.

It is most important that fish be provided with suitable places to live. Poor farm practices that silt our streams and lakes; pollution from industries, cities, and insecticides; and the destruction of natural watersheds and wetlands—these are the greatest enemies of good fishing today.

**TAGGING FISH** helps biologists learn how rapidly fish grow, how far and how fast they travel, and other facts. Return tags to address given and describe where and when catch was made.

**CANOES** are lightweight, portable boats, averaging 16 to 18 ft. long. Designed to be used with a paddle but may be driven with outboard. Fiberglass, aluminum, or canvas over wood.

**PUNT or JOHNBOAT,** with square, upswept bow, is stable and draws little water. To 24 ft. long, of wood planking or aluminum. An ideal boat for float fishing on rivers.

**BOATS FOR FISHING** are selected for use rather than looks. Though almost any kind of boat can be used, a good fishing boat should have plenty of open space for casting and for playing fish. No single type of boat is best for all kinds of fishing. Some waters are fished best from a boat propelled by oars, paddle, or push-pole. Larger waters may require use of a motor to save traveling time or to cover more water, as in trolling. In some states, boats must be registered and licensed in the same manner as automobiles. Your boat or outboard dealer can give you specific information. Many fishing boats—skiffs, utility boats, and even cruisers—have live wells built into the hull. Portable units are also available. Holes in the bottom of a live well allow water to circulate and keep it fresh. Used mainly to store live bait but also to keep catch alive.

**ACCESSORIES** help make boat safer, more comfortable. Coast Guard regulations require life preservers or approved cushions. Folding seats, which may swivel 360°, are restful and excellent for trolling.

**SKIFF** has flat bottom, high bow. A stable boat, 10 to 16 ft. long, designed to be rowed but may be used with small outboard motor. Of wood planking, plywood, or aluminum.

**UTILITY BOATS,** up to 18 ft. long, are wide, with rounded or V-shaped bottom. Propelled by outboards, they are best all-purpose fishing boats. Of wood, fiberglass, or metal.

**CRUISERS,** powered by inboard or outboard motors, are larger boats for offshore fishing or for "camping out" on the water. Many have twin engines for greater speed and safety. Ranging in length from 18 to over 40 feet, they may be luxuriously furnished. Some have kitchens, sitting rooms, and even air conditioning. The best type for fishing has a small cabin and a large, open cockpit for plenty of fighting room. Cruisers are made of wood, fiberglass, steel, or aluminum.

**ANCHORS** used by fishermen are: (1) Mushroom, named for shape, holds well in soft mud bottom. (2) Navy, good all-around anchor with hinged flukes. (3) Danforth, with large hinged flukes, holds fast but is easy to dislodge.

# OTHER SOURCES OF INFORMATION

BOOKS can help in identifying fish and also give details about particular kinds of fishing. Those listed below are general. Available, too, are books that treat particular places, kinds of fishing, or species, such as bass, trout, salmon, and others.

Boschung, Herbert T., Jr., et al, *Field Guide to North American Fishes, Whales, and Dolphins* (Audubon Society), Alfred A. Knopf, New York, 1983.

Elman, Robert, *The Fisherman's Field Guide*, Ridge Press, Alfred A. Knopf, New York, 1977.

McClane, A. J., *McClane's New Standard Fishing Encyclopedia and International Angling Guide*, Holt, Rinehart, and Winston, New York, 1974.

McNally, Tom, *Fishermen's Bible*, Follet Publishing Co. Chicago, 1970.

Migdalski, Edward C. and George S. Fichter, *Fresh and Salt Water Fishes of the World*, Alfred A. Knopf, New York, 1976.

Sparano, Vin T., *Complete Outdoors Encyclopedia*, Harper and Row, New York, 1980.

Zim, Herbert S. and Hurst H. Shoemaker, *Fishes*, Golden Press, New York, rev. ed. 1987.

MAGAZINES with regular information on sport fishing include *Outdoor Life, Field and Stream, Sports Afield,* and *The Salt Water Sportsman*.

CATALOGS of many sporting goods companies describe latest tackle and equipment, and many contain helpful hints and tips. Names and addresses of the companies can be found in the ads in outdoor magazines.

CONSERVATION DEPARTMENT publications give information about fishing regulations and about places to fish. Address questions to Conservation Dept. (or Fish and Game Dept.) at your state capitol.

# INDEX

Asterisks (*) denote pages on which illustrations appear.

159

MEASURING SCALE (IN INCHES)